LITERACY
REFRAMED

How a Focus on

Decoding, Vocabulary, and

Background Knowledge

Improves Reading Comprehension

ROBIN J. FOGARTY   GENE M. KERNS   BRIAN M. PETE

With Jan Bryan & Cheryl Ballou

555 North Morton Street
Bloomington, IN 47404
800.733.6786 (toll free) / 812.336.7700
FAX: 812.336.7790

email: info@SolutionTree.com
SolutionTree.com

Visit **go.SolutionTree.com/literacy** to download the free reproducibles in this book.

Printed in the United States of America

Library of Congress Cataloging-in-Publication Data

Names: Fogarty, Robin, author. | Kerns, Gene M., author. | Pete, Brian M., author.
Title: Literacy reframed : how a focus on decoding, vocabulary, and background knowledge improves reading comprehension / Robin J. Fogarty, Gene M. Kerns, Brian M. Pete ; contributors: Jan Bryan, Cheryl Ballou.
Description: Bloomington, IN : Solution Tree Press, 2021. | Includes bibliographical references and index.
Identifiers: LCCN 2020017028 (print) | LCCN 2020017029 (ebook) | ISBN 9781951075132 (paperback) | ISBN 9781951075149 (ebook)
Subjects: LCSH: Language arts. | Reading--Phonetic method. | Vocabulary--Study and teaching. | Reading comprehension.
Classification: LCC LB1576 .R623 2021 (print) | LCC LB1576 (ebook) | DDC 372.6--dc23
LC record available at https://lccn.loc.gov/2020017028
LC ebook record available at https://lccn.loc.gov/2020017029

Solution Tree
Jeffrey C. Jones, CEO
Edmund M. Ackerman, President

Solution Tree Press
President and Publisher: Douglas M. Rife
Associate Publisher: Sarah Payne-Mills
Art Director: Rian Anderson
Managing Production Editor: Kendra Slayton
Production Editor: Miranda Addonizio
Content Development Specialist: Amy Rubenstein
Copy Editor: Jessi Finn
Proofreader: Elisabeth Abrams
Text and Cover Designer: Laura Cox
Editorial Assistants: Sarah Ludwig and Elijah Oates

To Mortimer J. Adler, author extraordinaire of *How to Read a Book* and founder of the Great Books Foundation.

To humorist Mark Twain, who said,
"A classic is something that everybody wants to have read and nobody wants to read."

To our print- and digital-savvy readers; we hope you will remember these words of Mortimer J. Adler's:

"The goods of the mind are information, knowledge, understanding and wisdom."

"In the case of good books, the point is not to see how many of them you can get through, but rather how many can get through to you."

Acknowledgments

We want to acknowledge Mike Schmoker; E. D. Hirsch Jr.; Doug Lemov, Colleen Driggs, and Erica Woolway; and Daniel T. Willingham. These voices combined to become the spark of inspiration for this project.

As well, the influence of professional mentors who believed in us lingers. Here, we wish to share our gratitude for several of these voices from the past. Robin salutes two reading gurus: (1) Chris Rauscher, her mentor, who challenged her with the simple question, "What is reading?" and (2) Sylvia Ashton-Warner (1963), for her seminal teaching as author of *Teacher*. Both greatly influenced her teaching philosophy.

Gene addresses the topic of literacy with remembrance of and respect for the passion his friend and mentor, Terry Paul, had for the topic. He also gives thanks for his dear Aunt Bess, who spent hours reading and rereading him his favorite Little Golden Books, with him on her lap, at the beginning of his literacy journey.

We also want to thank friends and colleagues who are part of an ongoing dialogue and provide their honest, timely, and brilliant suggestions as they chat about, read, edit, contribute to, critique, and generally support our obsession *du jour*. Robin likes to try things out on Julie Constanza and Kathleen Mazurowski, soul-sister educators immersed in reading matters.

"Gene's team" of expert academic colleagues Jan Bryan, Cheryl Ballou, and Carol Johnson have been standby writing team members. In fact, Jan and Cheryl have become official contributors to this work, focusing primarily on the informative and sorely needed discussion of digital reading. Their names appear prominently on the cover for their timely contributions.

Brian acknowledges his oldest brother, Michael, who, when home from his freshman year of college, taught him not how to read but *how to read a book*—how and why to peruse the table of contents, scan the headings, interpret the introduction, and have a clear objective of why he was reading the book and what he expected to learn.

Lastly, publishers, editors, proofreaders, and graphic artists put their blood, sweat, and tears into the nitty-gritty mechanics of making a book. Indebted to the many brilliant craftspeople who influenced some aspect of the acquisition and production of this book, we are thankful to our favorite publisher, Douglas Rife; our go-to editor, Kendra Slayton; and the many graphic designers, editors, proofreaders, marketing wizards, and, last but not least, salespeople who all worked together to get this book into the hands of teachers.

Solution Tree Press would like to thank the following reviewers:

Sandy Jameson
English Teacher
Nazareth Area High School
Nazareth, Pennsylvania

Melissa Kaasa
Kindergarten Teacher
Roy Elementary School
Yelm, Washington

Visit **go.SolutionTree.com/literacy** to download the free reproducibles in this book.

Table of Contents

About the Authors

 **Robin J. Fogarty, PhD,** is president of Robin Fogarty & Associates as a leading educational consultant. She works with educators throughout the world in curriculum, instruction, and assessment strategies. Working as an author and consultant, she works with students at all levels, from kindergarten to college. Her roles include school administrator, and consultant with state departments and ministries of education in the United States, Puerto Rico, Russia, Canada, Australia, New Zealand, Germany, Great Britain, Singapore, South Korea, and the Netherlands.

Robin has written articles for *Educational Leadership*, *Phi Delta Kappan*, and the *Journal of Staff Development*. She is author of *Brain-Compatible Classrooms*, *10 Things New Teachers Need to Succeed*, and *Literacy Matters: Strategies Every Teacher Can Use*. She is coauthor of *How to Integrate the Curricula*, *The Adult Learner: Some Things We Know*, *A Look at Transfer: Seven Strategies That Work*, *Close the Achievement Gap: Simple Strategies That Work*, *Twelve Brain Principles That Make the Difference*, *Nine Best Practices That Make the Difference*, *Informative Assessment: When It's Not About a Grade*, *Supporting Differentiated Instruction: A Professional Learning Communities Approach*, *Invite! Excite! Ignite! 13 Principles for Teaching, Learning, and Leading, K–12*, and *The Right to Be Literate: 6 Essential Literacy Skills*. Her work also includes a leadership series titled *From Staff Room to Classroom: The One-Minute Professional Development Planner* and *School Leader's Guide to the Common Core*. Her most recent works include *Unlocking Student Talent: The New Science of Developing Expertise* and the second edition of *How to Teach Thinking Skills*.

Robin earned a doctorate in curriculum and human resource development from Loyola University Chicago, a master's in instructional strategies from National Louis

University, and a bachelor's in early childhood education from the State University of New York at Potsdam.

To learn more about Robin's work, visit www.robinfogarty.com or follow @robin-fogarty or @RFATeachPD on Twitter, Instagram, or Facebook.

Gene M. Kerns, EdD, is a third-generation educator with teaching experience from elementary through the university level and K–12 administrative experience. He currently serves as vice president and chief academic officer of Renaissance Learning.

With nearly twenty years of experience of leading staff development and speaking at national and international conferences, Gene has helped clients that include administrators' associations across the country, the Ministry of Education of Singapore, London's Westminster Education Forum, and the Global Education Technology Forum of China.

Gene received his bachelor's degree and master's degree from Longwood University in Virginia, and also holds a doctorate of education from the University of Delaware with an emphasis in education leadership.

To learn more about Gene's work, follow him on Twitter @GeneKerns.

Brian M. Pete is cofounder and CEO of Robin Fogarty & Associates. He has followed a long line of educators—college professors, school superintendents, teachers, and teachers of teachers—into a career in education. He has a rich background in professional development and has worked with adult learners in districts and educational agencies throughout the United States, Europe, Asia, Australia, and New Zealand.

Brian has an eye for the teachable moment and the words to describe skillful teaching. He delivers dynamic, humor-filled sessions that energize the audiences of school leaders, teachers, and teacher leaders with engaging strategies that transfer into immediate and practical on-site applications.

Brian is coauthor of *How to Teach Thinking Skills Within the Common Core, From Staff Room to Classroom: A Guide for Planning and Coaching Professional Development, From Staff Room to Classroom II: The One-Minute Professional Development Planner, Twelve Brain Principles That Make the Difference, Supporting Differentiated Instruction: A Professional Learning Communities Approach, The Adult Learner: Some Things We Know, A Look at Transfer: Seven Strategies That Work, School Leader's Guide to the Common Core, Everyday Problem-Based Learning: Quick Projects to Build*

Problem-Solving Fluency, Unlocking Student Talent, and *The Right to Be Literate: 6 Essential Literacy Skills.*

Brian earned a bachelor of science from DePaul University in Chicago and is pursuing his master's degree in fiction writing from Columbia College in Chicago.

To learn more about Brian's work, visit www.robinfogarty.com, or follow @brian pete or @RFATeachPD on Twitter, LinkedIn, Instagram, or Facebook.

To book Robin J. Fogarty or Brian M. Pete for professional development, contact pd@SolutionTree.com.

Preface

Our journey with this book started the moment Gene called Robin and Brian and asked, "Do you have a few minutes? Well, maybe more?" He piqued their curiosity as he began his pitch: "This is about the reading challenges that almost nobody's talking about." He was talking about supporting and advocating for a revolutionary shake-up in traditional reading protocols based on re-emerging and newly emerging research evidence. That phone call and exciting news set the journey in motion.

K–12 students in 21st century classrooms face reading challenges that few on the modern school scene are talking about yet. These challenges have only become visible as a consensus of ideas from four voices in education. First, the wisdom of school-improvement expert Mike Schmoker's (2018) *Focus: Elevating the Essentials to Radically Improve Student Learning* and his plea to prioritize the essentials of teaching and optimize the power of student learning both struck the right chord with the three of us. Second, American educator E. D. Hirsch Jr.'s (2018) tome *Why Knowledge Matters: Rescuing Our Children From Failed Educational Theories* broke new ground and fanned the flame of knowledge as the quintessential ingredient for reclaiming students' literacy legacy. Third, Doug Lemov, Colleen Driggs, and Erica Woolway (2016) advanced a phenomenal approach to instruction in their book *Reading Reconsidered: A Practical Guide to Rigorous Literacy Instruction*, boosted by, finally, psychologist Daniel T. Willingham's (2017) *The Reading Mind: A Cognitive Approach to Understanding How the Mind Reads*.

These last two books made us clearly and urgently decide to combine their ideas in ways that matter to teachers. We discovered how their ideas coincide with our aim to revisit common reading instructional practices (which have always included instruction on phonics, or *decoding*, and vocabulary development) and the critical role of content knowledge. This mingling of ideas contains the essence of a newly formed truth: massive amounts of time for authentic reading are necessary across all subjects in order for teachers to willingly release students to read successfully as a lifetime pursuit.

That's the story of *Literacy Reframed: How a Focus on Decoding, Vocabulary, and Background Knowledge Improves Reading Comprehension.*

Introduction

It is impossible to overstate the importance of literacy. Yet nothing so begs for clarity in K–12 education.

—Mike Schmoker

Imagine, in a year devoid of major financial market disruption, you dutifully invested twice the amount you did the previous year into your retirement account only to see that your account balance remained the same at year's end. You doubled down on your investment strategy, and it made no difference. How long would you continue that same approach?

Or imagine working overtime hours only to find the bottom line of your paycheck remained flat. Would you question the extra time you put in? Of course you would. Would you work overtime the next week? Likely not.

We want to know that our investments of time and energy pay reasonable dividends. Well, it's time for us to be honest and admit that we have a major literacy problem in U.S. education; we have expended vast amounts of resources and have little to show for it. It appears that our current approach to literacy is flawed, yet we continue to make huge investments that pay little to no returns.

The Massive Literacy Challenge Nobody's Talking About

As we track the evolution of reading instruction, we can think of it as a journey, a long and arduous experience for those educators who have witnessed its iterations since the 1960s. Teachers have earnestly instructed students in the customs of the day, from the earliest days of the one-room schoolhouse and the McGuffey's Readers taught by rote reading and writing; to reading instruction that relied heavily on sight words and the look-say method of published pre-primers and primers on the Sally,

Dick, and Jane sagas; to the upper-level basal texts, often themed for grade-level interests; to the 21st century's newest approach, the science of reading. Yet, in all this time, reading performance has barely improved and at times educators have seen catastrophic results (Joyce, Calhoun, & Hopkins, 1999).

Policymakers and educators alike acknowledge that literacy is the key to all learning, and we know that raising a student's literacy abilities increases scores across the content areas (Cromley, 2009; Martin & Mullis, 2013). This is intuitive and, in addition, English language arts (ELA) and literacy scores have been part of nearly every high-stakes accountability initiative; funding for literacy matches that priority. We educators focus on and fund literacy efforts. But the power of the academic dialogue does not match our results. Why? Perhaps, as Schmoker (2011) suggests, literacy is one of those essential things that we talk a lot about "but we have never fully clarified" or "obsessed over [its] implementation" (p. 9).

The perceived remedy was to focus on accountability for poor performance that began in earnest with President George W. Bush's No Child Left Behind (NCLB, 2002) initiative, which reauthorized the Elementary and Secondary Education Act of 1965. In turn, schools have become increasingly focused on an assessment-driven thrust toward reading achievement. In fact, the focus on skill-based approaches—referenced in our work as *overskillified models*—has had a monopoly in literacy instruction. Generous blocks of time for literacy were intentionally scheduled soon after No Child Left Behind to increase reading proficiencies across the grades. Unfortunately, in practice, teachers used these blocks for skill-and-drill workbooks and worksheets, as well as strategy lessons, devouring precious time set aside for improving the complex act of students authentically reading with fluency and comprehension.

> Schmoker (2011) suggests literacy is one of those essential things that we talk a lot about "but we have never fully clarified" or "obsessed over [its] implementation" (p. 9).

The detrimental effects of this focus on overskillification, unfortunately, have been wide reaching. In the following sections, we'll discuss how overskillification has caused literacy development to flatline and how research evidence has revealed a startling solution. People in schools, not just in ivory towers, are beginning to reassess and reframe how they will approach reading in the future.

A Flatlining Pattern

So, what do data say is the worst effect of existing unproductive literacy practices? Succinctly stated, it's stunted reading growth after the late elementary years. One of the most commonly used measures of text complexity, used to evaluate both the difficulty of books and the reading abilities of students on the same scale, is the

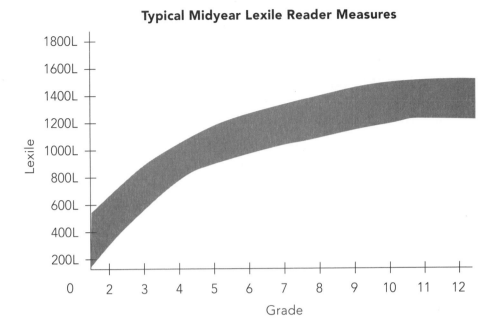

Typical Midyear Lexile Reader Measures

Source: MetaMetrics, n.d.

Figure I.1: Typical midyear Lexile reader measures.

Lexile Framework created by MetaMetrics. Figure I.1 depicts typical midyear Lexile measures across grades 2–12 for U.S. students ranging in performance from the 25th percentile to the 75th percentile (MetaMetrics, n.d.). In other words, this figure illustrates how a vast number of our students grow in terms of literacy.

What we see is consistent growth in the early grades that levels off quite substantially in the later grades. To some degree, this is a normal pattern for cognitive development and not necessarily a cause for immediate concern. Students often see very large reading gains in the early years; the difference between a student's reading skills in first grade and his or her reading skills in second grade will always be greater than the difference in the student's reading skills between tenth and eleventh grades. That said, it is a sad state of affairs when the difference in ability between seventh grade and twelfth grade is negligible. These five additional years of schooling typically do not increase most students' abilities to engage with more difficult texts.

Other data sets reflect this flatlining pattern. For example, the National Center for Education Statistics (NCES) stores the results of the National Assessment of Educational Progress (NAEP) online where anyone can search (www.nationsreport card.gov). Figure I.2 (page 4) uses a selection of these data to show stagnant reading proficiency rates across decades according to the years the test was administered (NCES, n.d.a, n.d.b, n.d.c).

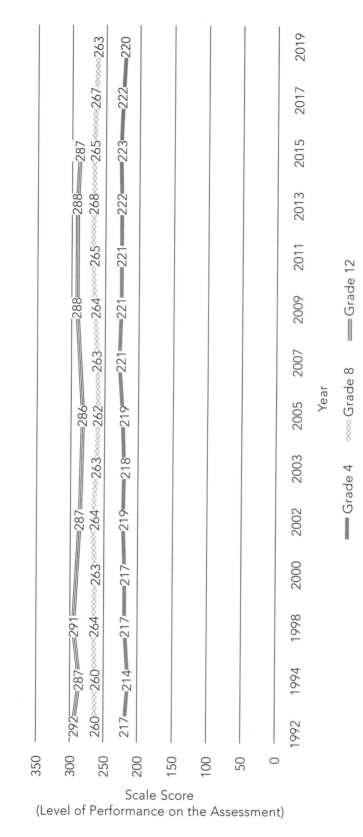

Source: NCES, n.d.a, n.d.b, n.d.c.

Figure I.2: National Assessment of Educational Progress reading score chart.

In our years of observing these data, we have seen that in most states, the highest rates of proficiency occur on third-grade reading tests, and then fewer students are proficient by the end of fifth grade, and still fewer in eighth grade and tenth grade. Over the years of school, proficiency rates drop considerably, and the gap between the highest- and lowest-performing readers gets wider. On some level, many educators have recognized this pattern, and sadly—whether consciously or unconsciously—they have, in essence, accepted it.

Understanding the predictive implications of whether a student can read on grade level by the end of third grade, more than thirty-five states have enacted programs designed to ensure just that—third-grade students read on grade level before the school year ends, according to Renaissance Learning (n.d.). Some of these programs include significant accountability measures such as retention. For example, Florida is one state that follows this protocol and in fact, does retain third graders who do not meet the ELA standards by the end of the year. If students achieve proficiency in reading in third grade, that's wonderful. But if they then fall behind by fifth, eighth, or tenth grade, the race is clearly not won—that is, they leave our schools noticeably unprepared and lacking the essential literacy skills of reading, writing, speaking, and listening. As Hirsch (2006) notes:

> It's in later grades, 6–12, that the reading scores really count because, after all, gains in the early grades are not very useful if, subsequently, those same students, when they get to middle school and then high school, and are about to become workers and citizens, are not able to read and learn proficiently.

We need to frankly discuss the fact that we cannot determine college and career readiness solely with third-grade scores. The illiteracy problem is endemic and demands our undivided attention.

There is another piece of this flatlining story that we must acknowledge. When NCLB was enacted in 2001, many schools reacted by cutting time devoted to science and social studies to increase time for the assessed areas of ELA and mathematics. Researcher Jennifer McMurrer (2007) notes there was a "47 percent reduction in class time devoted to subjects beyond math and reading" (as cited in Hirsch, 2018, p. 61). By increasing our efforts in the name of literacy, did we see any substantive changes in proficiency? No. And this reality should cause us to re-examine everything.

Continually stagnant rates of proficiency when many schools *substantially* increased time devoted to ELA clearly tell us that the way we are currently addressing literacy simply is not paying adequate dividends. Hirsch (2018) suggests that our current approach must be a "misconceived scheme," as "the 'accountability' principles based on [it] have not induced real progress in higher-level reading competence" (p. 28).

This brings to mind the familiar definition of *insanity* often attributed to Albert Einstein but actually written by novelist Rita Mae Brown (1983)—doing the same thing over and over and expecting different results. Since the 1960s, education communities have been acting insanely. The "reading wars" debate about the best way to teach reading (whole language versus phonics) did not help, nor did the billions of dollars in spending authorized through NCLB's literacy program Reading First, nor did the major reallocation of our most precious resource, time. We desperately need some new insights and actions around literacy. As professor of education David Steiner (2017) asserts:

> Stagnant student performance that leaves some 60 percent of high-school graduates unprepared for postsecondary training or schooling, the persistence of racial and socioeconomic achievement gaps, and the seeming futility of reform efforts all suggest that American public education is badly in need of a new path forward. (p. 11)

Stagnant rates of literacy stifle schools' ability to meet their modern mission. As assessment expert Rick Stiggins (2017) notes, schools could historically function as a mechanism for "sorting students into the various levels of our social and economic system" (p. 19). But that was the old mission. Today, schools are charged with "mak[ing] sure 'every student succeeds' at mastering fundamental reading, writing, mathematics, problem solving, and other proficiencies that they will need in this increasingly complex and fast-changing world" (Stiggins, 2017, p. 21). Schools cannot fulfill this mission with current approaches.

In a nutshell, the time has come for us to forthrightly address the prevailing literacy failure rate in our schools. Many school practitioners involved with aspects of reading and literacy across their curriculum probably know in their hearts that we have been nursing a failing mission. Administrators, principals, teachers, parents, and certainly the students themselves are aware of the predicament students are in when they can't, don't, or won't read. Too many of our students find themselves in this situation. Yet the same inadequate literacy instruction prevails, year after year.

We talk about the problem of failed reading scores all the time, we think about it, and we try to accommodate it, but to positively address it requires a massive shift. No one has taken this disaster in hand by moving the multiple, necessary working parts from the community, district, school, and home. We can't afford to be naïve about how radical the necessary changes are. We compare the shift to the children's game Fruit Basket Upset; in the game when a player calls out the words of the game's name, everyone must move to a different seat. We're talking about changes that impact existing schedules, curriculum, instruction, and assessment structures throughout the schooling community. A credible revamping of the literacy conundrum will take a village. There are already pockets of success in literacy achievement that are often attributed to superintendents with the right goals for their students, principals who champion literacy goals, extraordinary reading directors leading with common sense, and naturally, dedicated teachers who live by Rick DuFour's mantra, "Whatever it takes" (DuFour, DuFour, Eaker, & Karhanek, 2004). Like them, we believe in a fail-proof school, a safe haven to nurture literate young people and ready them for the ever-changing, ever-challenging world that awaits them. We strive to create schools where everyone can read fast, write well, speak clearly, and listen attentively, a backpack they can then take along on their life journeys.

Researchers Jared Myracle, Brian Kingsley, and Robin McClellan (2019) conclude, "Alarm bells are ringing—as they should be—because we've gotten some big things wrong: Research has documented what works to get kids to read, yet those evidence-based reading practices appear to be missing from most classrooms." How do we bring real change to an enormous, powerful, and deeply entrenched institution like K–12 education in the United States? This book presents the solution.

The Solution

While the broad K–12 education community is just truly beginning to acknowledge the reality of long-term flatlining reading performance, the research community has been waiting for educators to wake up. According to Myracle et al. (2019), "Literacy experts have been recommending the same research-based approaches since the 2000 National Reading Panel report, yet there still aren't systemic mechanisms for ensuring this information reaches the educators who set instructional directions," with "systemic failures having left educators overwhelmingly unaware of the research on how kids learn to read." Education journalist and author Natalie Wexler (2018) claims that much of our current approach is based on assumptions about how students learn that research has disproven, such as the need to teach lists of vocabulary words. We will delve into research throughout this book. The education world, however, hasn't yet paid much attention to these findings (Wexler, 2018).

The good news is that there is a substantial body of evidence, which we will share more fully throughout these pages, suggesting that we can address this phenomenon in knowledgeable ways. But it will require reframing our approach to literacy acquisition in terms of both policy and practice. Reading and writing success, as we will show, is fueled by the very performances we desire—that is, lots of reading and writing. But teachers must orchestrate reading and writing throughout the K–12 instructional day. This is no easy task. Our mission is big. Are we ready to finally end the reading wars, truly rely on evidence, and transition to ways of advancing literacy that actually pay dividends? If we are to have any chance of taking more students to a higher level of performance, substantive changes in our approach are required.

"I find it helps if instead of calling it an assignment
you refer to it as a 'must read.'"

Source: © Mark Anderson, www.andertoons.com. Used with permission.

A Distillation of Reading Comprehension

We clearly want students to continue to grow in their ability to comprehend successively more difficult texts. Yet before we go further, let's nail down exactly what reading comprehension is. For something so central to all academic success, remarkably, many of us, as educators, struggle to define it or explain it in any detail greater than saying, "It's when you understand what you read." How students learn to read may well be the most thoroughly researched area in education, yet our explanations of reading comprehension are tragically simplistic. In fact, at times, comprehension has been known as a *phantom skill* (Fogarty, 2007), meaning that we talk about it, reference it, write about it, and even test, retest, and score students on it, yet we seldom, if ever, define it succinctly. In short, comprehension is the ability to make sense of text by processing the code of language, understand its meaning, and integrate it with prior knowledge.

Nebulous definitions of comprehension hint at a fundamental problem that we must resolve if we are to ever have a highly literate populace. If we have a limited ability to describe reading comprehension, then it is highly unlikely that we will effectively guide students to master the ability to decipher meaning from coded language with consistency and precision. How do we arrive at the appropriate destination if we do not know precisely where it is?

As we discuss the true aspects of comprehension and how to foster them, you will likely find that you are doing a lot of good things that this book suggests you do in the classroom (such as read-alouds, voice and choice books selected by readers, buddy reading, vocabulary spotting, and accountable independent reading). You may also find that some things you are doing may in fact hinder the process of comprehension (for example, too much focus on worksheets, workbooks, isolated skill development, teacher talk, and sustained silent reading without sufficient checking for understanding).

Also, it's important to remember that some students are so profoundly advantaged by outside factors, such as having the opportunity to read voraciously on their own time, that they acquire advanced reading comprehension despite what teachers do or don't do. And other students, less advantaged, have little chance of success unless we significantly advance our ability to describe reading comprehension—the destination—in detail and learn how to effectively guide all students there. For these students, we must create multiple, quality opportunities to read with a partner for the needed support, use digital tools so they will use auditory stories, and even take time to do more oral reading with them so they hear the sound of language.

While we are suggesting that educators need to shift their focus from skill-based reading routines to meaning- or knowledge-based efforts, we want to make it very clear that we are not blaming educators for their choice of where to focus. Reform and regulatory requirements are certainly impactful. Author and cognitive neuroscientist Stanislas Dehaene (2009) places a good portion of the blame on policymakers and decision makers who "swing back and forth with the changing winds of pedagogical reform, often blatantly ignoring how the brain actually learns to read" (p. 2). Hirsch (2018) remarks that it is unfair that "teachers are being blamed for the poor results of this system" because "teachers have been misinformed about the actual nature of reading comprehension" (p. 75). In addition, leaders sometimes seem to imply that teachers must use all of the elements of the reading program supplied by the publisher. This may not be the case, but teachers will do whatever they think is expected of them.

When we consider the professional literature about reading comprehension as a whole, we find the usual suspects that are featured in this text, but with fundamental perspectives that make all the difference. We see phonics as a necessary first step to decoding written language; vocabulary, word choice, phrasing, sentence structure, and graphics as the visual input to help readers interpret meaning; and perhaps most important, background experiences, prior knowledge, emerging knowledge, and of course, the new knowledge revealed as understanding, meaning, and making sense are achieved. A survey of the professional literature reveals a common refrain: multiple authors discuss the same elements as critical and sometimes-overlooked factors contributing to reading comprehension (Hirsch, 2003; Lemov et al., 2016; Willingham, 2017). We present the elements here as the *big three*.

1. **Decoding:** Can you decipher the text? Can you use phonics to sound out unknown words? If so, how fluently?

2. **Vocabulary:** Do you know all the words in the text? If not, what percentage is unknown to you? Can you use context clues to help?

3. **Knowledge:** Do you have the necessary background knowledge to understand the context of and references in the text? Do these things make sense to you?

Let's explore each of these elements individually, and then see how they work together.

Decoding First

Although we associate phonics with the early years of reading, even adult learners use these skills when they encounter unknown words. Consider the word ОДеЯЛО. Can you decipher it? This is the Russian word for "blanket." Imagine you were a Russian preschool student; you would certainly know the word verbally, but if you had no phonetic knowledge of how to interpret the letters reflected in the word—no way to convert them to sound and meaning—you would be no closer to reading comprehension with this word than any of us with no knowledge of Russian.

Some of this word's characters have familiar elements, but overall, most of us English speakers will look at this word and have absolutely no idea how to pronounce it. We might assume that the word ends with a "-row" sound, but we are also a little unsure of several of the ending characters. Is an inverted R pronounced differently than a regular R? And we have likely never seen anything like the second letter of this word unless we have taken Russian.

Clearly, readers need to be able to efficiently convert the symbols of reading into sounds and meanings, but we would be remiss if we associated phonics and decoding with direct access to comprehension. For phonics to instantly aid us in comprehension, we must already know the word. If we sound out a word and have never heard it before, we are no closer to comprehension. This brings us to the next element, vocabulary.

Vocabulary Forever

Conversations about the importance of vocabulary are endless. Teachers in every subject area or discipline value the vocabulary of their content and often issue student lists of discipline-specific, academic vocabulary. Indeed, vocabulary plays a critical role in understanding. Hirsch (2018) asserts that "vocabulary size is the single most reliable correlate to reading ability" (p. 48). From this, we can conclude that the words we know profoundly affect and accurately predict what we will be able to read and comprehend.

Vocabulary is so critical when seeking understanding that readers "have a pretty low tolerance for reading unknown words. . . . Just how much unknown stuff can a text have in it before a reader will declare mental overload and call it quits?" (Willingham, 2017, p. 90). It turns out that, while estimates vary among researchers, and comprehension depends on the reader's attitude and motivation, the consensus is that readers need to know nearly all the words—98 percent—in order to comfortably comprehend what they're reading (Willingham, 2017). Every standards document that we know of includes some ELA standard that requires students to use context clues to guess the meaning of unknown words, but without sufficient context (more than 98 percent known words), determining the meaning of unknown words is virtually impossible.

> *Every standards document that we know of includes some ELA standard that requires students to use context clues to guess the meaning of unknown words, but without sufficient context (more than 98 percent known words), determining the meaning of unknown words is virtually impossible.*

So, with decoding ability and vocabulary, we are getting much closer to comprehension. However, these are only two of the big three. Without knowledge—the last element of the big three—it is possible for students to know how to decode all the words in a text and know what they mean, and still not comprehend what the author is trying to convey.

Knowledge Foremost

Let's turn to "the most recently understood principle" of literacy: knowledge (Hirsch, 2003, p. 12). To understand why knowledge may be necessary even when you know all the words in a text, take a look at the following list of words.

- *belonging*
- *call*
- *category*
- *contained*
- *intuition*
- *manifold*
- *means*
- *mine*
- *necessary*
- *represented*
- *self-consciousness*
- *synthesis*
- *understanding*
- *unity*

You should be able to easily decode and define all these vocabulary words. You have two of the big three literacy elements covered. Armed with your decoding and vocabulary abilities, read the following short passage from Immanuel Kant's (1781/1998) *Critique of Pure Reason*, and try to correctly answer the low-level question asking for basic recall on the passage's main idea:

A manifold, contained in an intuition which I call mine, is represented, by means of the synthesis of the understanding, as belonging to the necessary unity of self-consciousness; and this is effected by means of the category.

The main idea of this passage is:

    a. Without a manifold, one cannot call an intuition "mine."

    b. Intuition must precede understanding.

    c. Intuition must occur through a category.

    d. Self-consciousness is necessary to understanding.

    (Hirsch, 2006)

While some philosophy majors with adequate exposure to Kant's work might have easily read the passage and correctly answered the corresponding question, many of us probably floundered, because we lack this background knowledge on Kant. Perhaps, in reading the passage, you felt like the elderly lady from a commonly told anecdote about Einstein. She attended a lecture on relativity given by the famous scientist, and afterward, she approached him and remarked, "I understood all the words. It was just how they were put together that baffled me" (Hirsch, 2003, p. 17). Hirsch (2006) critiques teachers' tendency to try to teach reading comprehension skills by simply giving struggling readers more time to summarize, classify, and find the main idea, which he says these readers cannot possibly do without the necessary background knowledge.

To fully comprehend the provided passage, we need to know that Kant was deeply interested in how people perceive the world (intuition) through organizing mind-sets, paradigms, or *manifolds* that they build over time based on their experiences. Combining this knowledge with our decoding and vocabulary abilities gets us much closer to the correct answer: C.

Willingham (2017) advances that background knowledge is a primary cause of flatlining reading scores: "Students from disadvantaged backgrounds show a characteristic pattern of reading achievement in school; they make good progress until around fourth grade, and then suddenly fall behind. The importance of background knowledge to comprehension gives us insight into this phenomenon" (p. 128).

We could summarize our entire discussion so far with the following statement, which reflects the big three: after one has learned the mechanics of reading, "growth depends, more than anything, on our ability to build up students' knowledge base and vocabulary" (Schmoker, 2018, p. 27). And so now we turn our attention to how the three elements interact.

The Synergy Required for Comprehension

While it is helpful to analyze the elements of decoding, vocabulary, and knowledge separately to fully understand each of them, we must also realize that they interact like factors in an equation, the result of which is comprehension. In fact, missing elements in literacy cause the same kind of imbalance that comes with a missing element in an equation. Remember what happens when you multiply by zero. You could have all the knowledge needed to comprehend a text you are reading, and you could know all the text's words verbally, but if you don't know the phonics of the text, you'll multiply by zero, and the result is zero comprehension. Similarly, you could know how to decode the words of the text and know all their meanings, but without sufficient background knowledge, you will again multiply by zero, and the result is zero comprehension.

In contrast with a reader who struggles to decode words, advanced readers recognize them in milliseconds. For truly literate individuals, the elements of the big three blend seamlessly. Nearly instantaneous recognition is accompanied by equally instant association with meaning, and advanced readers have the knowledge to fully understand the context. The result is comprehension.

"Students from disadvantaged backgrounds show a characteristic pattern of reading achievement in school; they make good progress until around fourth grade, and then suddenly fall behind. The importance of background knowledge to comprehension gives us insight into this phenomenon" (Willingham, 2017, p. 128).

The Overskillification of Reading

Willingham claims that "the mistaken idea that reading is a skill—learn to crack the code, practice comprehension strategies—may be the single biggest factor holding back reading achievement in the country" (as cited in Schmoker, 2011, p. 102). He and Schmoker (2011) note that "once students begin to read, they learn to read better by reading—just reading—not by being forced to endure more reading skill drills" (p. 103). And Lemov et al. (2016) point out simply, "Excellence in almost any academic subject requires strong reading" (p. 1).

Consider the construct of the Common Core State Standards (CCSS) for ELA (National Governors Association Center for Best Practices [NGA] & Council of Chief State School Officers [CCSSO], 2010), which devotes countless pages to listing the various skills within the standards, while a mere four pages, scattered throughout, address specific content. The standards leave the ultimate decisions of what knowledge to impart up to the schools. This makeup is in no way unique to the CCSS.

Most other standards sets have the same dynamics: lots of discrete skills listed, with only passing references to specific knowledge. Is it any wonder, then, that teachers view literacy as a collection of various skills? Cognitive scientists and psychologists, however, take a very different view.

This reliance on skills is a very common theme emerging in the professional literature, which we will refer to as the *overskillification* of reading. This results in two dynamics, neither of which is helpful. First, overskillification encourages teaching reading skill by skill, rather than understanding that students achieve comprehension through many interdependent skills and abilities. Second, requiring students to learn lengthy lists of skills often precipitates numerous skills-based lessons that, sadly, take more and more time away from students actually reading. It's like a football practice where you spend all your time doing worksheets and watching videos about specific skills, at the cost of actually taking to the field and integrating the skills in a scrimmage or actual game situation.

"Excellence in almost any academic subject requires strong reading" (Lemov et al., 2016, p. 1).

Reading comprehension strategies are an excellent example of overskillification. As Schmoker (2018) asserts, "Symbolism, figurative language, setting, mood, or structure have their place but are absurdly overemphasized in state standards" (p. 125) at the cost of truly authentic literacy. Daniel T. Willingham and Gail Lovette (2014) note that direct instruction on reading comprehension strategies does make a statistically significant difference in general reading performance, but they also note these skills "are quickly learned and don't require a lot of practice." They expressly state that there are "plenty of data showing that extended practice of [reading comprehension strategy] instruction yields no benefit compared to briefer review." Hirsch (2006) notes that "six lessons in comprehension strategies yield as much or as little benefit as 25 lessons," meaning that educators must be aware of the beneficial but "very limited efficacy of strategy-practicing." As a result, Willingham and Lovette (2014) call for educators to "curtail English language arts activities that offer the smallest payout," noting that "strategy instruction may have an upper limit, yet building background knowledge does not." We can conclude, then, that spending too much time on these strategies simply takes time away from just letting students read and develop their personal schema of background knowledge to build on.

We are not saying that instruction on specific skills or strategies has no impact. It does; it's just that your return on time investment diminishes quickly. According to reading researchers Anne Castles, Kathleen Rastle, and Kate Nation (2018), "The benefits of strategy instruction appear to emerge after relatively little instruction: There is little evidence that longer or more intensive strategy interventions lead to greater improvements in reading comprehension" (p. 35). That's where the time becomes available for significantly more student reading. Similarly, Hirsch (2018) notes:

"I've paraphrased, summarized, outlined, compared, contrasted, and inferred. Can I just read now?"

Source: © Mark Anderson, www.andertoons.com. Used with permission.

> Students do show an initial positive effect from practicing finding the main idea. But their progress quickly reaches a limit and then halts. We know this from various meta-studies as well as from the stagnant NAEP data. Drills in formal comprehension skills have not raised mature reading scores; rather, they have taken up a lot of class time that could have been devoted to knowledge building. (p. 20)

The ability to find a main idea or make an inference is a manifestation or byproduct of comprehension. Students do not read well because we have taught them the hundreds of skills reflected in the standards. They are able to perform those skills because we have taught them to read well by focusing on the big three.

Now armed with the big three elements as a distillation of comprehension, we teachers best know where to focus. Decoding, vocabulary, and knowledge are truly the essence of comprehension, not all the individual reading comprehension skills and strategies that occupy so much of our time.

The Journey Ahead

Now that we have a better understanding of what comprehension is, we can begin to fully explore how to develop it. We need to consider how teachers can best promote the process of literacy acquisition, but our findings will not merely be about what teachers must do. If we are going to make substantive changes in student performance, we must also come to understand how students not only can but must become self-teachers in the process. There is work they must do, and we must create the conditions for that to happen.

First of all, let's mention why we've chosen to title the book *Literacy Reframed*. Our ambition with *Literacy Reframed* is to reframe K–12 teachers' approach to literacy, moving from a skill-based frame to a more holistic and knowledge-centric one. A knowledge-centric approach to reading values the actual knowledge one receives from reading. Knowledge learned is the ultimate takeaway from the literacy experience. We intentionally use the word *reframe* because we are putting a brand-new frame on the existing picture of literacy. It is about changing perspectives, or educators' view of the endgame of reading. Teachers can then use this reframed vision of literacy to craft enduring learning for aspiring readers.

In visual arts, particularly cinematography, framing is the presentation of visual elements in an image, especially the placement of the subject in relation to other objects. When we frame a scene in a different way, the new frame doesn't change the contents of the picture, but it changes the focus of the person viewing the picture. Framing can make an image more aesthetically pleasing and keep the viewer's focus on the framed scene. One example from the visual arts is the framing technique *repoussoir*, or the use of an object near the edge of a composition that directs attention into the scene. In French, *repoussoir* means "pushing back" ("Repoussoir," n.d.); this book pushes teachers' attention away from the distractions that have plagued them and back to what matters. Basically, our aim is to give teachers a sense of the value of knowledge and meaning instead of letting them rely so heavily on students' skillfulness as readers. The painting "The Art of Painting" (https://bit.ly/3ddHped) by Johannes Vermeer (1666–1668) demonstrates *repoussoir*; a curtain in the foreground gives the audience only a partial view into an artist's studio, but frames that view so that viewers see the studio in a certain way.

By the way, if you stumbled upon the word *repoussoir* and did not know what it means, you would probably try to figure it out by sounding it out in your head, relying on what you learned about phonics in the first grade. You would also probably try to define it considering the context of how it was used. If you were completely unfamiliar with the word, you would naturally look up the definition in the dictionary (or simply google it). Regardless, the point is that you would use techniques you learned in elementary school to help you develop your vocabulary. You would consider the context in which the word was used, look up the word, and consider synonyms you might know, using the lifelong skill of vocabulary building while continually expanding your personal word bank. And finally, you would look for examples of the word in the real world to build a deeper understanding or knowledge base about the visual arts. It seems pertinent to mention that the ability to conduct this kind of search for context clues develops over time when one has spent a lot of time just reading. Rich, relevant reading pays dividends with advancing literacy. This idea exemplifies not the overskillification of reading but the totality of reading comprehension, literacy acquisition, and the big three elements under scrutiny.

In illuminating a dynamic new path forward that reframes our perspective on literacy, *Literacy Reframed* devotes a chapter to each of the big three elements of reading comprehension. Chapter 1 covers decoding and discusses the *sound* of literacy and phonics. The sound of language awakens students' sensitivities from an early age. In chapter 2, we move on to vocabulary, concentrating on the *look* of literacy. The look of language includes the images of letters, of words with tall letters and letters that hang down, of a string of words called a phrase, sentence, or question, and even of the graphic configurations of paragraphs, dialogue, and poetry on the page or screen. Words seem like mere squiggles to students at first but ultimately become familiar and identifiable to the youngest readers. The element of knowledge appears in chapter 3, which focuses on the *knowingness* of literacy—that is, background knowledge. The knowingness of language involves students' brains making sense of the sound and sight of language to continually build their mental map of background knowledge.

Finally, we have devoted chapter 4 to digital reading. In this age of technological innovation, digital reading takes its rightful place in the *Literacy Reframed* landscape. We felt it was important to include a chapter on this important topic because the model of paper-and-pencil reading and writing is now juxtaposed with digital devices of every size and shape in our learning environments. We aim to distill the essence of digital reading concerns within the frame of the school, classroom, and students. Digital literacy combines the sound, look, and knowingness of literacy in unique ways, and we feel it's essential for teachers to acknowledge and use these similarities and differences as they work toward the overall goal of educating literate young people and making them ready to enter the wide, wide world of known and unknown challenges.

In each chapter, we begin with a brief introduction and an overview of the essential research. Then we transition to ideas for school implementation and classroom applications of a knowledge-centric curriculum in a variety of grade levels and subjects.

We close each chapter with a list of team discussion questions and essential resources that readers can use to extend their learning. For schools that function as professional learning communities (PLCs), these questions are perfect for collaborative team meetings to help build trust, establish cohesive goals, and learn from one another (DuFour, DuFour, Eaker, Many, & Mattos, 2016). Our goal is to steer teachers toward some new ways to use our ideas throughout their literacy curriculum work, regardless of the subjects they teach.

Chapters 1–4 at a Glance

As educators, we must aim to change the frame on our old, static, failed picture of reading growth. We need a new perspective on literacy learning, with massive amounts of reading and writing for success. The evidence is clear that much more reading and writing inspire student confidence and ensure their success. We must rally students to the call for literacy learning every day, in every way. The following hypothetical classroom vignettes illustrate how teachers could go about teaching reading with a reframed perspective on literacy.

Chapter 1: The Sound of Reading—Decoding and Phonics

Marilyn Ferguson (1980) writes, "Language releases the unknown from limbo, expressing it in a way that the whole brain can know it" (p. 80). In the following vignette, note the inextricable connection between the words people say and the words they write. It highlights the connectedness of our models of language.

Mrs. Lathers asked her eleventh graders, "How do you know what you think until you see what you say?" This question helped students think about the revelations that naturally occurred as they began to write. The oral language they heard in their heads came out a bit differently when they wrote their ideas on paper. In fact, they found that the words they wrote came out more formal than the words they said to themselves, but because it was their own writing in their own words, they found it easy to read. This is part of the differences we often encounter in the verbal voice and written voice. It's what Ferguson (1980) is describing when she talks about releasing the unknown from limbo. We know that experience with spoken and written language radically restructures the brain, especially for the very young (Boroditsky, 2019). In fact, it is how the brain learns, literally, by changing its chemistry and its structure to capture the concept through the natural neurological activity of learning.

The multimodal learning process in the brain is alerted with the *neurological-impress method*, a technique pioneered by clinical psychologist R. G. Heckelman (1969) that involves a student and a partner reading aloud simultaneously from the same book. This method allows students to see, say, and hear fluent language, and this combination of senses helps them decode unknown words. To impact students' reading levels, teachers should foster plenty of opportunities for students to speak, listen to, and write vocabulary.

Chapter 2: The Look of Reading—Vocabulary

The look of reading is intriguing. The different ways that readers can perceive the look of what they're reading means they make distinctions and choices. Marilyn Ferguson (1980) writes, "The mind aware of itself is a pilot" (p. 69). Readers can use their self-awareness of the look of reading to note the choices they make and how they react to what they notice about what they read. In the following story, see how students' journey of choosing a book to read independently can embody this idea.

Ms. Sutton wanted her fourth graders to pick out a book to read on their own during silent reading time in class. During a trip to the school library, she asked them to make their choices based on what the books look like. The look of reading can cause students to prejudge many aspects of reading choices. A student might think, "I love the cover," "It looks like a big-kid book 'cause it's so thick," and "The pages are completely covered with words; no places to stop and start. No pictures. It bet it's going to be hard; definitely a long slog, so here goes."

The look of reading is in the mechanics and the aesthetics. If a word doesn't look right, it could be a spelling error. If a text has shorter paragraphs, with openings of white space or a graphic or callout to interrupt the text, it's more inviting to the reader. The look of a poem, a passage, or even a run of dialogue offers a break in text for the weary reader. Knowing this to be true, talk about reading choices with your students. Get them thinking about how they think about the look of a reading.

Chapter 3: The Knowingness of Reading—Background Knowledge

Eric Hoffer (1973) points out, "In times of drastic change it is the learners who inherit the future. The learned usually find themselves equipped to live in a world that no longer exists" (p. 22). We see this quote as a comment on the rapid changes that occur in all sectors of the world, including education, and the need for swiftness when moving on to the newest methods. Those not able to make the shift will be left behind. But without background knowledge, there is nowhere to shift from. The brain builds on background knowledge that's already present and makes neurological adjustments to fit the incoming messages into existing patterns. This is the story of learning: building on existing knowledge in a dynamic way and chunking information to make sense of it and store it for logical recovery when needed. The following vignette concerns the essence of what *knowing* is all about. It's that metacognitive moment when we call on our brain to work deeper.

When Mr. Ellington repeated, "You know more than you think you know. Your brain is smarter than you," these sixth-grade students knew to think again, to

continued ▶

search for connections that made sense of the content they were reading. In fact, Mr. Ellington actually heard students saying under their breath, "I know; I know more than I know I know." This behavior was more obvious when they deciphered an optical illusion or discerned the patterns in a tessellation or laughed aloud at a cartoon image that seemed hilarious the instant it registered on the brain. It was clear when they finally had that break, that rare aha moment, that they knew he was right.

A truth to take away: It's important and intelligent to know what we know and what we don't know.

Chapter 4: Digital Reading

What could be better, in a world of information amid misinformation, than a digital reader in your back pocket?

This story is our ode to the technology advancement that allows us to revisit and refresh the background knowledge stored in our brain. It's called the *computer*, whether a tiny handheld device, a tablet, or a desktop processor, it's a ready, fast backup like an ever-ready battery.

Mr. Hass's seventh-grade students were digital-savvy readers, each with a smart-phone near at hand. Rather than having to go to the dictionary in the corner or yell out, "What's a thesaurus?" these students had a *background knowledge center* with them at all times. He coached, "When you're stumped, think in your head first to see if you can recover any ideas. If not, then ask your partner, and finally, dig out the digital wizard and search with Siri or google it to find the answer on your own."

One's body of knowledge is enhanced by background experiences and prior understanding. When a chunk of knowledge is missing, the brain searches for a connection. Teachers who understand the power of knowledge-driven reading understandably value the use of a digital device.

Along the way, we will explore some closely related ideas such as the emerging requirements around assisting dyslexic students sooner, the impact of transitioning to digital texts, and the potential for literacy acquisition to support the acquisition of social-emotional skills.

The topic of literacy is highly charged, with skirmishes from the so-called reading wars somehow still persisting. We have tried to fully substantiate each claim herein with solid research, rather than any particular philosophy or preference. In doing this, we respectfully interpret the work of Mike Schmoker, Daniel T. Willingham, Stanislas Dehaene, E. D. Hirsch Jr., and other respected voices in the field of literacy instruction, including Isabel Beck, Rick Stiggins, Doug Lemov, and more. They have powerful insights to share, and based on long-term performance metrics, we are eager for some new thinking about how to best teach literacy, and even more eager to put the innovations into practice.

As the famous lyricist Oscar Hammerstein II suggests, "Let's start at the very beginning / A very good place to start" (Rodgers & Hammerstein, 1965). His lyrical start was for learning to sing in *The Sound of Music*. Let us begin with the sound of literacy.

CHAPTER 1

The Sound of Reading—
Decoding and Phonics

*Reading to students from the math book has a demystifying impact
on the miracles and mysteries of math.*

—Anonymous

When twins Mike and Mitch hear their mom yell out, "Oh no!" the boys instantly start guessing what's happened. Mike thinks the "Oh no!" is an exclamation of surprise: "Maybe she is pleasantly surprised about our new arrangement of the garage, since she's using that high-pitched, sing-song voice."

"No way!" Mitch says. "That was not her high-pitched, pleasant-surprise voice; that was her very loud, 'Oh no, I'm mad, and I can't wait to tell you how furious I am' voice. She's not at all happy about the garage. I don't think she wanted all the bikes, rackets, and camping gear hung up on all three walls."

Mike says, "Let's find out."

Mitch replies, "You first."

This story emphasizes the inherent power of voiced words. This situation should sound familiar because it illustrates how sensitive we humans are to sounds. A child's earliest recognitions are the many nuanced sounds of the human voice. Children hear sounds and register the volume, tone, and tenor in their attempts to make sense of the world. Slowly, they begin to understand the sounds as words and associate meanings with them (Diamond & Hopson, 1999). All of this happens naturally with spoken language, but there is nothing natural about learning to interpret the symbols of written language. This is where decoding and phonics come in.

Playful Phonics and the Sound of Literacy

Much like you might open a lesson with a playful, thought-provoking exercise to allow students to warm up before the real work begins, we deliberately begin each chapter of this book by referencing something fun about the key elements of literacy.

This chapter about the many sounds of literacy starts off with some tongue twisters and other word fun to ignite mindful thinking (searching for connections) and creative mental meanderings (seeking words that have specific sounds). In turn, you can share these passages with your students. For each of these examples, you might display one or two lines at a time and let your students take their cues from you as you and they say the words.

The Sound of Letters

Say the letter sounds emphasized in the alliteration of tongue twisters:

> Peter Piper pick'd a peck of pickled peppers. . . .
> Where's the peck of pickled peppers Peter Piper pick'd? (Harris, 1836, pp. 51–52)

The Sound of Words

While reading a poem, say the emphasized word sounds:

> Sarah Cynthia Sylvia Stout
> Would not take the garbage out! (Silverstein, 1974, p. 71; see https://bit.ly/3hOlk7A for full poem text)

The Sound of Phrases

Working in pairs, complete the stem phrases in the following list:

"Have you ever . . .? What if . . .? Why not . . .? Coming . . . "

The Sound of Sentences

Say the stem and complete the famous literary opening (Mumford, 2015) with your own thoughts:

"It was a dark and stormy night . . ."

The Sound of Narrative

We all remember stories; that's one reason nursery rhymes so readily remain in memory.

> Jack and Jill went up the hill
> To fetch a pail of water;
> Jack fell down and broke his crown,
> And Jill came tumbling after. (Wright, 1916, p. 49)

> **The Sound of Nonfiction**
>
> Read aloud Newton's (1846) three laws of motion, one at a time.
>
> 1. Every object persists in a state of rest or in a state of movement forward as compelled by its state of force impressed.
>
> 2. The alteration of motion is ever proportional to the motive force impressed in the direction of the right line in which force is impressed.
>
> 3. Every action has an opposite and equal reaction, and objects remain at rest or continue to move at a constant velocity unless acted upon by a force.

Phonics: How to Teach It Effectively

Let's look a little closer. When we talk about decoding, what we're getting at is phonics. Teachers of older students may dismiss that term at first glance, but as we'll discuss, phonics has a place throughout grades K–12.

What exactly is phonics? In a nutshell, *phonics* involves specific and discrete elements that include *phonemes*, or units of sound, and the letters of the English alphabet, including vowels and consonants as well as *blends* (such as *sk-* or *cl-*) and *digraphs* (such as *ch-* or *ph-*). In short, phonics centers on the early literacy skills of associating the sounds and symbols of language (Watson, 2019).

What Phonics Curriculum Encompasses

Curriculum should encompass the following six aspects of phonics.

1. Forty-four phonemes (the smallest part of spoken language) and two hundred eighty-four graphemes (the smallest part of written language)

2. Sequence for introducing letter-sound correspondences—a, m, t, s, i, f, d, r, o, g, l, h, u, c, b, n, k, v, e, w, j, p, y, T, L, M, F, D, I, N, A, R, H, G, B, x, q, z, J, E, Q (Carnine, Silbert, Kame'enui, Slocum, & Travers, 2017)

3. The twenty-six letters of the English alphabet—*a, b, c, d, e, f, g, h, i, j, k, l, m, n, o, p, q, r, s, t, u, v, w, x, y,* and *z*

4. The five or six vowels—*a, e, i, o, u,* and sometimes *y*

5. The twenty or twenty-one consonants—*b, c, d, f, g, h, j, k, l, m, n, p, q, r, s, t, v, w, x, z,* and sometimes *y*

6. Blends and digraphs

While phonics instruction dominates early reading lessons, when teachers necessarily break down oral language and the sound of reading into the letter-sound relationships, it does continue throughout the learning years. As students learn to decipher the sounds of language, phonics directly follows the analytical parts of literacy learning through the elementary grades as an important element of reading, writing, and spelling.

Phonics is still definitely present in the intermediate- and secondary-grades curriculum in some form, with a focus on root words, prefixes, suffixes, derivatives, and, in more sophisticated measures, the actual sounds of words and strings of words and the tone, tenor, and nuances of the music-like sounds of language. At these more sophisticated levels, students learn to appreciate word choice, dialogue, and dialect in scripts; writing style; and the emotional tension in well-written pieces.

Teachers can nurture students' reading lives by making sure they have a solid phonics foundation. In the following sections, we'll explain that teachers must make sure phonics programs have structure and sequence, use phonics as a bridge to successful reading, be aware of the limitations of phonics instruction, and move beyond mechanics to the next phase of literacy acquisition.

Create Phonics Programs With Structure and Sequence

Foundationally, instruction on the phonics used to decode words is about the relationships between the letters of written language and the sounds of spoken language. Teaching students about these relationships is important because it leads to an understanding of the *alphabetic principle*: the systematic and predictable relationships between written letters and spoken sounds.

Programs of phonics instruction are effective when they are *systematic*. The plan of instruction includes a carefully selected set of letter-sound relationships that are explicitly organized into a logical sequence. The programs provide teachers with precise directions for teaching these relationships. Effective phonics programs provide ample opportunities for students to apply what they are learning about letters and sounds, and use them to read words, sentences, and stories. Systematic and explicit phonics instruction that significantly improves students' word recognition, spelling, and reading comprehension is most effective when it begins in kindergarten or first grade.

Elementary level students must learn phonics with brief bursts and then apply their learning immediately, with coaching feedback, to reach a level where decoding words is automatic and habitual. Of course, how teachers conduct this instruction matters. The emerging approach of *deliberate practice* is distinguished by its hallmark features of short, frequent, and intense sessions in which students read the same passage multiple times and take frequent breaks to recover; this is what is known as *reach and repeat*. Anders Ericsson and Robert Pool (2017) stress these elements in their evidence-based work on deliberate practice. It is the best way to foster best practices in place of the skill-and-drill regimen of the past (Ericsson & Pool, 2017). Teaching phonics in an effective sequence will significantly influence the rate at which students successfully acquire phonics knowledge and skills.

As stated earlier, the sound of literacy is where language begins. Human beings are prewired to learn language by hearing it spoken. Dehaene (2009) notes, "At the age of five or six, when children are exposed to their first reading lessons, they already have an expert knowledge of phonology. They also possess a vocabulary of several thousand words and have mastered the basic grammatical structures of their languages" (p. 198). All of this has occurred with little or no formal instruction.

In most cases, any "reading" that students do prior to formal instruction is actually what German psychologist Uta Frith (1985) refers to as the *pictorial phase* of literacy acquisition (as cited in Dehaene, 2009). During this phase, children look at words exactly as they do objects or faces, perceiving words exactly as they perceive pictures. Words are merely entire images with which they have become familiar. They know some very familiar words purely through repeated exposure (for example, their name or a famous brand, such as the Coca-Cola scripted text logo). This concept is critical, and we will more fully discuss it in subsequent sections.

Suggestions for Ideally Structured Phonics Instruction

At the phonological level, preschoolers benefit from playing with words and their component sounds (syllables, rhymes, and finally phonemes).

At the visual level . . . the Montessori method, which requires tracing sandpaper letters with a fingertip, is often of considerable assistance . . . [in] figuring out each letter's orientation, and makes it clear that b, p, d, and q are different letters.

Children must be taught, without fear or repetition, how each letter or group of letters corresponds to a phoneme (sound).

Because English spelling is complex, introductions of graphemes (visuals) must occur in logical order.

Children's attention must be drawn to the presence of these individual elements within familiar words. This can be done by assigning each grapheme a distinctive color, or by moving them around to create new words.

The ability to attend to the various subcomponents of words is so essential that this must be taught explicitly, for instance, by covering words with a sliding window that reveals only a few letters at a time.

Going too fast can also be a handicap. At each step, the words and sentences introduced in class must only include graphemes and phonemes that have already been explicitly taught.

Source: Dehaene, 2009, pp. 228–229.

Phonics Is the Logical Bridge Into Reading

When everything young students know about language is based on sounds and they must transition to a world of print, phonics serves as the most logical bridge. It takes them from the words they already know verbally to the ability to read them visually. Literacy scholar David L. Share (1995) notes that phonics instruction represents "the logical point of entry since it offers a minimum number of rules with the maximum generative power" (p. 156). As a result, "any plausible model of reading acquisition must assign phonology a leading role" (Share, 1999, p. 95). Phonology comprises all the sounds of a word that students are trained to hear and to reproduce. It's important throughout the continuum of phonics instruction as the human ear becomes highly sensitive to barely audible variations in sounds.

Research on the effectiveness of phonics instruction is clear as exemplified in this sense: "Phonics approaches have been consistently found to be effective in supporting younger readers to master the basics of reading" and are "more effective on average than other approaches to early reading" (Pimentel, 2018). Similarly, a research summary from Britain's Education Endowment Foundation (n.d.) notes the research base for phonics as having "very extensive evidence," and its highest rating. Language arts standards expert Susan Pimentel (2018) suggests that "it is not an overstatement to say that a school that doesn't have a phonics program is doing its students a huge disservice." It is one of the key elements in the foundation of phonics instruction.

Highly critical of many other 21st century education policies, multiple authors view the increased emphasis on explicit and systematic phonics instruction driven by changes to standards and accountability since 2010 as an improvement in U.S. schools' literacy efforts. Hirsch (2018), for example, remarks, "The testing regimens have clearly helped improve the mechanics of early reading," which he views as "an important gain" (p. 11). With so much emphasis on reading in the early grades and having students reading on grade level by the end of grade 3, schools have thoughtfully reviewed their curricula and attempted to ensure that their programs are research based. As a result, more students are now receiving the explicit and systematic phonics instruction that research validates.

Though a strong proponent of phonics instruction, Dehaene (2009) does address the concerns of whole-language advocates by stating, "Learning the mechanics of reading is not an end in itself—in the long run, it only makes sense if it leads to meaning" (p. 229). In summary, he remarks:

> As a scientist and a professor myself, I expect the teachers and educators to whom I entrust my children to invest as much obsessive care in the design of lessons as my colleagues and I do when we prepare a psychological experiment. (Dehaene, 2009, p. 230)

The groundwork for further development of reading excellence is carefully laid out with the stepping stones of phonics instruction. Dehaene's (2009) words capture the idea of an approach to phonics instruction that is direct (explicit) and carefully crafted (systematic).

The phrase *the science of reading* has begun to appear in the professional literature with increased frequency. This basically means ensuring that the instructional approaches that teachers use are based on the very best research-validated methods. Phonics is one such element that has run the gamut of scientific studies with levels of positive findings that qualify as proof of its effectiveness. We suggest, however, that some may be limiting the science of reading solely to phonics.

Borrowing from a perspective Willingham (2017) offers in *The Reading Mind*, we assert that there are multiple sciences of reading. We find his presentation of the cognitive approach, one based on detailed studies of the brain's organization, operations, and reactions to various stimuli, highly useful but, as he notes, "That's not the only scientific perspective on reading" (Willingham, 2017, p. 9). For example, yet "another scientific literature employs the sociocultural view, which emphasizes the role of the social environment in reading" and "the cognitive approach is not in opposition to this view; it's just different" (Willingham, 2017, p. 9).

Strong proponents of phonics have, rightly so, gravitated to the science of reading, seeing it as a reflection of the broad, extensive research base supporting an appropriate phonological approach. Any author or publication, however, that presents phonics as the totality of the science of reading is portraying an incomplete picture. The extensive research base for literacy goes well beyond phonics.

Understand How Far Phonics Can Take Readers

Despite a powerful research base for phonics, many don't fully accept the primacy of its role in early reading. As Castles et al. (2018) note, "Despite extensive scientific evidence, accumulated over decades, for the centrality of alphabetic decoding skills as a foundation of learning to read, there remains resistance to using phonics instruction methods in the classroom" (p. 38). And, even though phonics provides most students with the optimum start in terms of literacy, we must acknowledge that phonics has limitations, and we must consider the wider landscape of literacy. As previously noted, phonics instruction represents "a minimum number of rules with the maximum generative power," but it has some appreciable limitations that we must acknowledge (Share, 1995, p. 156). Relying solely on phonics to read has appreciable drawbacks.

First, relying fully on phonics or decoding to read is exhausting. Having to decode too many unknown words saps so much cognitive-processing power that comprehension becomes impossible. Nearly every educator has observed a student expend so much energy on sounding out the words of a text that, at the end of the process, the student has read the words aloud but is unable to answer the most basic question about the reading. When this happens, the fluency of the reading process has been halted beyond repair or synthesis. Readers have finite processing power, and if decoding the words takes most of this power, then they have nothing left over to think about or even take in what they read. As "overtrained readers, [teachers] no longer have much perspective on how difficult reading really is," but for developing readers, the difficulty is quite real (Dehaene, 2009, p. 218).

Next, for phonics to be instantly helpful in terms of comprehension, readers must already know the meaning of the word they are sounding out. If you sound out a word and have never heard it before, you may be no closer to understanding it. Over time, readers do develop the capacity for self-teaching, eventually gaining the ability to "decipher the pronunciation of a novel string and associate it with a familiar meaning," but this capacity takes time to build (Dehaene, 2009, p. 226). This is why reading to students daily and exposing them to language and text are critical factors.

Finally, relying on phonics is certainly not what advanced readers generally are doing. To be clear, when they encounter a completely unknown word, advanced readers do revert to phonics, but the vast majority of the time they are recognizing words instantly by sight or through using their knowledge of known words to figure out at least parts of unknown ones. That said, we do explore more of what advanced readers do in subsequent sections.

Reading Is More Than Something Mechanical

At the heart of some concerns about phonics is a nagging feeling or core belief that reading is not purely mechanical, that it is more than a collection of phonetical abilities. But teachers struggle to clarify exactly what the *more* is, outside of catchphrases like *the joy of reading* or *getting lost in a story*. According to Castles et al. (2018), educators know that literacy is more than just skills, but there hasn't been much discussion of the actual evidence that this is so. As a result, "calls for a greater focus on phonics instruction can seem unbalanced" when they are not coupled with the larger considerations of the beauty and facility of language (Castles et al., 2018, p. 36).

In the end, any helpful conversation about phonics must clearly acknowledge that "the acquisition of phonics knowledge is by no means all there is to learning to read" (Castles et al., 2018, p. 16). It is quite possible to overemphasize phonics; more of a good thing isn't always better. A theme has emerged across the work of multiple authors that, while literacy instruction should begin with phonics, advanced literacy skills go far beyond this humble beginning. Researchers Philip B. Gough and Michael L. Hillinger (1980) and Rod Maclean (1988) note that "the spelling-sound correspondence rules to which a child is first introduced are very different from those he or she will eventually acquire as a skilled reader" (as cited in Share, 1995, p. 156).

Proponents of a whole-language approach will take solace in the Education Endowment Foundation's (n.d.) cautionary remark couched within its highly favorable review of phonics research:

> Teaching phonics is more effective on average than other approaches to early reading (such as whole language or alphabetic approaches), though it should be emphasized that effective phonics techniques are usually embedded in a rich literacy environment for early readers and are only one part of a successful literacy strategy.

Similarly, as Myracle et al. (2019) note, "Some express fears that phonics instruction comes at the expense of students engaging with rich texts, yet every good curriculum we know incorporates strong foundational skills and daily work with high-quality texts." It's about balance. "The National Reading Panel got it right: Literacy work is both/and, not either/or" (Myracle et al., 2019).

Becoming fully literate is analogous to taking a journey to a new, faraway land. Assume that getting there requires a flight and that the first step in getting to the airport requires exiting your driveway and turning right. Phonics instruction is that first right turn. That first turn is the correct, most efficient first step, but there's much more to the journey.

Go Beyond the Mechanics of Reading

Once again, when students in the early reader phase, at whatever grade, have learned the mechanics of reading, literacy acquisition naturally transitions to another, more sophisticated phase in which the primary drivers of growth are reading, being read to, and reading with others in small groups or with reading buddies. This would also include complementary writing exercises. Solid phonics instruction begins the process, but there is much more to becoming an advanced, avid, self-propelled reader.

While phonics begins students' literacy acquisition journey with a phase in which teachers directly instruct students on specific skills (such as letter-sound pairings and consonant blends), the next phase of literacy acquisition is one in which the teacher's role becomes secondary. In order for their literacy abilities to continue to grow and flourish, students must become capable of self-teaching, which we are about to explore in detail.

An acknowledgement of this second phase of literacy acquisition—the self-teaching phase—gives us a way to understand why reading growth flatlines. If we can come to better understand the elements of this phase, we can create conditions in which far more students can teach themselves much of what they need to advance their reading competencies. And it's critical that we do that because many of our struggling students should not be struggling. Many of them have all the skills and abilities necessary for success, but they fail to flourish because we do not know how to create the conditions for them to do so.

Share (1995) asserts that, when late elementary school students struggle, they usually fall into one of two categories: (1) students who have specific reading disabilities or (2) students who are "garden-variety struggling readers" (p. 186). The sad reality is that we produce a lot of garden-variety struggling readers. They represent the majority of readers who struggle. These students have challenges that "are not primarily attributable to . . . general intelligence, semantic or visual processes" (Share, 1995, p. 186). They have the ability; they just have not had the necessary experiences.

As we press forward, we will explore how to help these students flourish. And this begins by tapping into their innate ability to learn language by hearing it spoken and read to them.

Best Practice: Reading to Students—Crucial, but Often Neglected

Given the human propensity to take in language by hearing it spoken and the fact that having heard a word before facilitates decoding it, let us now explore the other aspect of the sound of reading: the critical need to read to students daily at all levels.

When parents, older siblings, and teachers read to very young children—toddlers, preschoolers, and primary-grade students—they can nourish the process of *preliteracy*, or the development of early behaviors and skills that lead to successful reading. At this point, learning takes place through a favorite bedtime story (*The Cat in the Hat* [Seuss, 1957], "The Song of Hiawatha" [Longfellow, 1909], "Jack and the Beanstalk" [Ottolenghi, 2002]), or often-repeated nursery rhymes. It should be fun and not feel like a chore. Heed the wisdom of children's book author and literacy expert Mem Fox: "When I say to a parent, 'read to a child,' I don't want it to sound like medicine. I want it to sound like chocolate" (Fox, 2008, p. 56).

As students enter their years of schooling, the importance of being read to does not diminish. Consider the following statements about the importance of reading aloud to students.

- In *Becoming a Nation of Readers*, Richard C. Anderson, Elfrieda H. Hiebert, Judith A. Scott, and Ian A. G. Wilkinson (1985) state, "The single most important activity for building the knowledge required for eventual success in reading is reading aloud to children" (p. 23).

- Literacy professor Steven L. Layne (2015) advances, "Those who know the research are aware of the consistent findings in regard to the benefits of reading aloud to children and young adults. It is best practice. It is sound practice" (p. 7).

- Former International Literacy Association president and Clemson University distinguished professor of education Linda B. Gambrell (personal communication, as cited in Layne, 2015) proclaims, "Reading aloud deserves to be a high priority in the literacy curriculum" (p. 46).

- Former International Literacy Association board member and professor at the University of Illinois at Chicago William H. Teale (personal communication, as cited in Layne, 2015) recommends, "The classroom practice of reading aloud should be a guiding principle for teachers at any level of our educational system" (p. 72).

- In *Invitations: Changing as Teachers and Learners K–12*, educator and author Regie Routman (1991) remarks, "Reading aloud should take place daily at all grade levels, including junior high and high school" (as cited in Layne, 2015, p. 8).

- Lemov, Driggs, and Woolway (2016) herald reading to students as "an integral part of any successful reading program in order to expose students to texts (and ideas!) significantly above their reading level, model fluent reading for students, and instill a love of reading and a love of literature in our students" (p. 239).

- Hirsch (2018) contends, "In the earliest grades learning by being read aloud to and through talking and listening is fundamental to language progress and needs to receive great emphasis" (p. 168).

Despite these experts' admonitions that teachers should regularly read aloud to students, we question how often they actually do so, particularly as students progress through the grades. Some question why, once students can read independently, teachers still need to read to them. There are many reasons, which we unpack in the following section.

The Language of Books

One of the most important reasons to read aloud to students is that "the everyday language that students hear does not prepare them to enter into the world of books, because both narrative and informational books represent *book language* that is very different from spoken language" (L. B. Gambrell, personal communication, as cited in Layne, 2015, p. 44). Why do authors use such drastically different language in written work? They need to do so because of the following:

> Speech usually takes place in a communicative context, meaning that some cues that are *present* in speech (e.g., prosody, gesture, tone of voice, facial expression) are *absent* in writing. To compensate, written language draws on a much larger vocabulary and more complex grammar: Noun phrases and clauses are longer and more embedded, and the passive voice, more formal voice is much more common. (Castles et al., 2018, p. 31)

With this understanding of how drastically different the typical written word is from the generally spoken word, teachers will either take the time to expose students to the advanced language of texts by reading to them, or fail to take this step and hope, against all odds, that students will somehow be successful when they encounter this unfamiliar world of advanced language on their own—an unlikely occurrence.

Another specific reason to read to students is that it facilitates other aspects of literacy acquisition. Educator and author Jim Trelease (2013) uses a metaphor of water flowing through various levees, as reflected in figure 1.1, to help us understand the critical need to read to students.

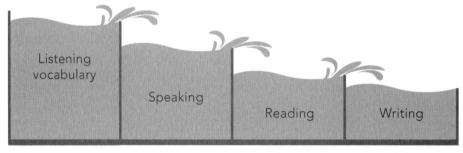

How can you speak, read, or write the word if you've never *heard* the word?

Source: Adapted from Trelease, 2013.

Figure 1.1: Speaking vocabulary, reading vocabulary, and writing vocabulary.

Trelease (2013) explains:

> The first levee would be the *Speaking Vocabulary*. You pour enough words into the child's Listening Vocabulary [by reading to him], and it will overflow and fill the Speaking Vocabulary pool—thus the child starts speaking the words he has heard. It's highly unlikely that you'll ever say

a word if you've never heard that word. . . . The next levee is the *Reading Vocabulary*. It's nearly impossible to understand a word in print if you've never said the word. And finally, there's the *Writing Vocabulary*. If you've never said the word or read the word, how in the world will you be able to write it? *All language arts flow from the Listening Vocabulary*—and that has to be filled by someone besides the child. Simple. (p. 14, emphasis added)

Additionally, reading to students not only fosters their reading abilities but also promotes their writing abilities. In *The Reader in the Writer*, authors Myra Barrs and Valerie Cork (2001) state, "Children who are read to in class write with more assurance, using a wider range of vocabulary, sentence structures and larger text structures than those denied this experience" (as cited in Layne, 2015, p. 47).

Beyond the logical case for reading to students, there's an equally powerful emotional one, particularly for students who were seldom, if ever, read to at home. Reading to students can create powerful positive associations with books. As Willingham (2017) notes, "Research shows that positive childhood experiences with books are associated with later reading" (p. 140). Furthermore, "Your reading attitude is mostly emotional. It's based on whether reading seems rewarding, excites you, or interests you. . . . Because reading attitudes are mostly emotional, logical appeals about the value of reading won't do much" (Willingham, 2017, pp. 138, 140).

Trelease (2013) positions reading to students as a commercial for reading that "conditions the child to associate books and print with pleasure" (p. 6). This is absolutely critical and irreplaceable, particularly for struggling students, because, as Trelease (2013) states:

> The learning experience can often be tedious or boring, threatening, and often without meaning—endless hours of work sheets, intensive phonics instruction, and unconnected test questions. If a child seldom experiences the pleasures of reading but increasingly meets its displeasures, then the natural reaction will be withdrawal. (p. 6)

Reading to students not only fosters their reading abilities but also promotes their writing abilities. In The Reader in the Writer, *authors Myra Barrs and Valerie Cork (2001) state, "Children who are read to in class write with more assurance, using a wider range of vocabulary, sentence structures and larger text structures than those denied this experience" (as cited in Layne, 2015, p. 47).*

And, yes, being read to is not just for early elementary students. It's for students at every level. Henrietta Dombey (personal communication, as cited in Layne, 2015), former president of the United Kingdom Literacy Association and professor emeritus at the University of Brighton, asserts, "Reading aloud gives older children a relaxation from the tension of competing school tasks and a shared experience of enjoyment" (pp. 46–47). Trelease (2013) bemoans the fact that:

> by middle school, almost no one is reading aloud to students. If each read-aloud is a commercial for reading, then a decline in advertising would naturally be reflected in a decline in students' recreational reading. . . . Unlike McDonald's, we often cut our advertising each year instead of increasing it. (Trelease, 2013, pp. 5–6, 38)

Finally, reading aloud to students creates incredibly fertile ground for phonics to work optimally. As Trelease (2013) notes, "As you read to a child, you're pouring into the child's ears (and brain) all the sounds, syllables, endings, and blendings that she will someday be asked to read and understand" (p. 14). This creates a dynamic where "students *know* words before they *read* them for the first time, and are then able to decode them more effectively" (Lemov et al., 2016, p. 242, emphasis added). By reading to students, teachers fill their listening vocabulary and prepare them to be effective as they enter the language of a book.

Read-Alouds in the Classroom

Reading aloud in the classroom is an opportunity to expose students to more challenging texts than they might otherwise encounter, but for this to be optimally effective, teachers must make informed choices about what to read. According to Lemov et al. (2016):

> On the too-infrequent occasions that teachers do read aloud to students, the text is often too simplistic. Read-aloud is a unique opportunity to breathe life into texts that students are unable to read independently [and it] exposes students to complex sentence structures and vocabulary and builds background knowledge. (p. 240)

Layne (2015) positions reading aloud as helping students in "listening up" (p. 55). He refers to the highly researched dynamic that "the listening level of a child (the level at which he hears and comprehends text) is significantly higher than his silent reading level" until the two converge around grade 8. This makes reading aloud "the medium for exposing those students to more mature vocabulary, more complex literary devices, and more sophisticated sentence structures than they would be finding in the grade-level texts they could navigate on their own" (Layne, 2015, p. 55). In consideration of all of this, Layne's (2015) general guidance is that teachers "consider selecting the majority of [their] read-alouds from texts written one to two grade levels above the grade level [they] are teaching" (p. 55).

Lemov et al. (2016) also advise teachers to practice their read-alouds ahead of time:

> A common mistake that teachers make in reading aloud to students is
> neglecting to practice. Simply picking the passage that you want to read
> for your students is not enough. Pick it and pre-read it—that will let you
> read it with flair. Reading is like making music. The notes and rests have
> different lengths, implicit in both how they are written and how they are
> interpreted. (p. 243)

These classroom read-alouds are an important way to help give students the exposure to language that they need to flourish. As Castles et al. (2018) note, "The process by which this transition from novice to expert word reader occurs is complex, and many questions remain" (p. 24). They lament a "relative lack of attention to aspects of reading acquisition that go beyond alphabetic decoding" and hint at what students need after "this initial knowledge of spelling-sound relationships that allows children to access the meanings of printed words and thus gain the text experience that is essential for the acquisition of higher-level reading" (Castles et al., 2018, p. 16).

These more advanced aspects of reading acquisition include voice, mood, tone, simple pronunciation, and articulation, as well as pacing, fluency, flow, and expression. These sophisticated nuances are accentuated when teachers read aloud to students, creating an inspiring experience with text. Reading aloud to students means that students get the advantage of having these things modeled for them regularly.

"I worked all week adding describing words to my story
and you knew the whole time I'd be illustrating it?!"

Source: © *Mark Anderson, www.andertoons.com. Used with permission.*

The Thirty-Million-Word Difference

Educational researchers Betty Hart and Todd Risley (1995), who intensely document the disparity of language experiences for young children (ages 7–36 months) across demographic groups, developed some of the most significant and highly cited work in the area of language acquisition. Their very laborious work involved visiting the homes of forty-two different families for extended periods across multiple years, recording parents' dialogues with their children, and then manually transcribing and analyzing those dialogues.

Their findings are often referred to as the *thirty-million-word difference*, which forms the basis of the book *Meaningful Differences in the Everyday Experience of Young American Children* (Hart & Risley, 1995). Their work reveals huge variances in the language experiences of preschool children that typically follow socioeconomic lines; children in more affluent households receive much more exposure to language than those in less affluent ones. They summarize some of their high-level findings:

> The data revealed that, in an average hour, some parents spent more than 40 minutes interacting with their child, and others spent less than 15 minutes. Some parents responded more than 250 times an hour to their child, and others responded fewer than 50 times. Some parents expressed approval and encouragement of their child's actions more than 40 times an hour, and others less than four times. Some parents said more than 3,000 words to their child in an average hour together, and others said fewer than 500 words. (Hart & Risley, 1995, p. xx)

The variance in experiences is immediately apparent from these numbers, but Hart and Risley (1995) call our attention to the cumulative totals and long-term effects of the gap, noting that "for each family, the amount the parents talked to their children was so consistent over time that the differences in the children's language experience, mounting up month by month, were enormous by age 3" (p. xx). Not surprisingly, they found that these experiences were closely tied to later academic outcomes. "With few exceptions, the more parents talked to their children, the faster the children's vocabularies were growing and the higher the children's IQ test scores at age 3 and later" (Hart & Risley, 1995, p. xx).

A more contemporary study sought to replicate the work of Hart and Risley (1995) but also apply more advanced technology than they had at their disposal. Jill Gilkerson et al. (2017) employed highly advanced recording devices developed by the LENA Foundation, a nonprofit that provides technology-based programs to accelerate children's language development. These devices allowed Gilkerson et al. (2017) to access full-day recordings of over three hundred families, resulting in a far larger sample size than Hart and Risley (1995) obtained, and avoiding the potential impact that a physically present researcher recording conversations might have on normal family interactions. Additionally, while Hart and Risley (1995) primarily focused on adult word counts, the LENA technology could quantify the adult word count, the child vocalization count, and the "conversational turn-taking counts," or dialogue (Gilkerson et al., 2017, p. 252).

Gilkerson et al. (2017) report that, though there were some differences, their data "generally corroborate the Hart and Risley (1995) findings, demonstrating quantitative differences among [socioeconomic-status] groups on some language behaviors measured over the course of the day" (p. 260). Their total word count variance, however, was not as large as that found by Hart and Risley (1995). They found that "children whose mothers graduated from college were exposed to 3,000 or so more words per day, translating into a four-million-word gap by 4 years of age between the highest and lowest [socioeconomic-status] groups" (Gilkerson et al., 2017, p. 260). Gilkerson et al. (2017) believe that this variance was primarily caused by the studies' different methodologies; they recorded fourteen-hour periods while Hart and Risley (1995) documented one-hour periods, "typically recorded during the early evening hours, which is a time of relatively high talk and interaction," which "likely resulted in inflated daily estimates" (Gilkerson et al., 2017, p. 261). Unique to Gilkerson et al. (2017) was the analysis of conversational turns. They found that "children in the most educated group typically engaged in over 50% more turns than those in the lowest group" (Gilkerson et al., 2017, p. 258).

In short, both studies reveal that, generally speaking, students from high-socioeconomic-status households typically are exposed to far more language and are involved in more conversational turns than their low-socioeconomic-status counterparts. Hart and Risley (1995) also document far more expressions of approval and encouragement for high-socioeconomic-status students. Schools serving disadvantaged students must make every effort to address their students' needs through exposure and access to text, as well as regular read-alouds.

The Phonics-Dyslexia Connection

While discussing the sound of reading, we would be remiss if we did not briefly address dyslexia. As education consultant and researcher Louisa Moats remarks, "The students who suffer most when schools don't give their students insight into the code [of phonics] are kids with dyslexia" (as cited in Hanford, 2018). "Dyslexic kids have to be taught to read more painstakingly, with special attention to phonemic awareness," as they have unique needs with the sound of reading, and they find the transition from symbols to sounds far more difficult than their nondyslexic peers do (Luscombe, 2019). Dehaene (2009) states that "current estimates indicate

continued ▶

that from 5 to 17 percent of children in the United States suffer from dyslexia" (p. 237). Though researchers have struggled to find a precise, physiological cause for this "peculiar deficit" that "affects the conversion of written symbols into sounds," Dehaene (2009) remarks it may actually have a variety of contributing causes, because "an activity as complex and integrated as reading necessarily lies at the intersection of multiple causal chains" (p. 242).

Dyslexia has a spectrum of manifestations, with some students being profoundly affected overall by the disability and others much more mildly so. Also, while there are some fairly common characteristics of dyslexia (see the following list), the disability's manifestations are so myriad that some students have no observable trouble with some specific characteristics but are profoundly impacted by others. When students struggle abnormally with or have low scores in multiple of the following areas, additional screening for dyslexia may well be warranted.

- Phonological awareness
- Phonemic awareness
- Letter knowledge
- Alphabetic principle
- Sound-symbol recognition
- Decoding
- Vocabulary
- Comprehension
- Reading accuracy
- Listening comprehension

Policy changes around dyslexia have happened amazingly swiftly. According to Belinda Luscombe (2019), editor-at-large of *TIME*, "A decade ago, just five states had any laws that mentioned dyslexia," yet, as of 2019, well more than forty do, with some specifically requiring that all students undergo screening for characteristics of dyslexia. Why the sudden uptick in policy? "Legal experts, teachers and literacy advocates point to one organization in particular: Decoding Dyslexia, a decentralized group of parents who have used social media and online resources to mobilize, raise awareness, and lobby state and federal legislators" (Luscombe, 2019). Their movement demonstrates the power of social media. Decoding Dyslexia chapters are now in all fifty U.S. states and Canada.

Many states do require that all students receive a screening for the characteristics of dyslexia. As a general rule of thumb, students who score in the bottom 25 percent on general outcome reading measures warrant a closer look. If they particularly struggle with the skills noted in the preceding list, additional testing to either confirm or exclude dyslexia would be advisable. And this testing might include a battery of measures, as dyslexia manifests in such varied ways.

This brings up the issue of screening for the characteristics of dyslexia versus diagnosing dyslexia—two fundamentally different things from an assessment and testing standpoint. The universal screeners for characteristics of dyslexia cannot diagnose it. The screeners are merely a first line of defense designed to be administered efficiently.

If students fall below a certain threshold (for example, the 25th percentile) on a universal screener and exhibit characteristics of dyslexia, then far more targeted and nuanced tests will be necessary to make a diagnosis, much like a doctor's assessment of a patient's blood pressure is a vital factor in a standard medical examination but not diagnostic in and of itself.

For dyslexics, the earlier a diagnosis comes, the better. When it goes undiagnosed, dyslexia can have a profound impact. Education journalist Grace Tatter (2016) notes that undiagnosed dyslexia "has been linked with higher rates of high school dropouts and even imprisonment and suicide." The link is correlated, not causal, but profound struggles in reading acquisition can easily precipitate all sorts of other issues. Because literacy skills are so vital to academic success in school, which students in turn easily tie to their own ideas of intelligence and self-worth, the impacts on dyslexics are not limited to literacy. They may also deal with low self-esteem, lack of confidence, less verbal interactions, seldom self-initiating interactions, or depression.

Along with the aforementioned emphasis in this book on implicit and systematic phonics instruction, multisensory approaches (combining sight, sound, and touch) seem particularly promising with the thought that such approaches help build necessary connections in the brain. In addition, dyslexic students often benefit from assistive tools such as audiobooks and note-taking tools.

Classroom Applications for Teachers

When students engage in decoding and phonics, we hear the sounds of literacy—the squealing voices of elementary-level students as they look through a picture book on the reading rug, their tones rising as they argue about one character in the story. Middle-level students gather around a table, leaning in rambunctiously and talking all at once as they brainstorm words they need to know to solve mathematics problems—*estimate*, *logical*, and so on. We also see students reading at their desks and talking about their daily paragraph, an assignment the teacher has given them as a bell-ringer activity that they can then finish throughout the day. Students are being read to, and they are reading to others; they are working on figuring out a word by separating it and sounding it out, and we hear one calling out to the room in general, "Who knows how to spell *spaghetti*?" These are busy, somewhat-noisy scenes, but when we listen closely, we hear that the words are the sounds of thinking minds.

Before we plunge into classroom practices that illuminate student reading in action, it seems prudent to specify the frame *Literacy Reframed* provides, which helps teachers consider how they can try out these practical scenarios in their classrooms. This frame shifts teachers' focus from a skill orientation to a knowledge orientation; it accentuates the rich and resounding elements that bring incredibly interesting and informative knowledge pieces to the forefront. In brief, *Literacy Reframed* envelops three angles of comprehension to bring reading alive: (1) the sound, (2) the look, and (3) the knowingness.

Fundamentally, literacy begins in the early elementary years with a traditional phonics program, yet it doesn't stop there in our treatment of the sound of language. Applications include a plethora of sounds in spoken language and listening experiences. All these auditory inputs contribute to the wholeness of language.

The following classroom scenarios at various levels truly illustrate what *literacy reframed* means. These inspired classrooms show subtle and not so subtle differences in shifting the reading scene to a highly visible and audible experience as students embrace the reading scene. Confidence is high, and students are reading together, alone, at their desks, on the rug, and at the computer and listening centers. It is busy and bustling; it represents a shift in perspective from a teacher-led, teacher-directed, and teacher-managed classroom to one in which students are the focus, comfortably owning their own learning. It is essential that we, as educators, study how the sound, the look, and the knowingness of reading instruction impact students' literacy throughout their learning years. To that end, this section includes knowledge-centric lessons about the sound of literacy for preK–3, 4–6, 7–8, and 9–12. The scenarios are based on real instances with composites of real teachers, thus, their names are appropriately fictionalized for the text.

Mrs. Clovis's First-Grade Class

In grades preK–3, phonics focuses on picture-rich visuals and a phonics toolbox for learning how to decode specific letter sounds into words. That gets students started with steps toward learning how to read. More specifically, early literacy includes three stages; first is a *pictorial* or *logographic reading stage* focused on students' seeing letters and words as they see objects and faces, and basically looking at the words as a whole or images as a whole. To illustrate a cognitive search for whole-picture identification, we've chosen an application called Chalk Talks. Second, the *phonological stage* (Willingham, 2017) signals when young readers start hearing the sounds of letters and words as phonics becomes functional. Third, the *orthographic reading process* takes place, when the look of reading and the sound of reading combine as parallel paths to unlocking the mystery of reading. A second classroom idea to try is the Sound Book, which helps guide students to go deeper and focus on one particular phonics sound.

Session 1: Chalk Talks

The first graders in Mrs. Clovis's class gather on the reading rug for one of their favorite parts of class. They are eager listeners, as they have been learning lots about the sound of language. As Mrs. Clovis begins, she tells them, "Today is a special reading treat, because I will have a job, and you will have one also. My job is to read and draw. Your job is to listen closely to the story and also to look carefully at the lines that I draw. As you look and listen, you will try to figure out what I am drawing. Frame by frame, you will hear and see things. Are you ready for the Chalk Talk?"

To back up a bit, a Chalk Talk is storytelling in its simplest form. It consists of ten original and individually complete draw-along tales written especially for early language learners. With each presentation, students listen in anticipation and watch in wonderment as the magically contrived narrative unfolds and the developing picture gradually emerges. Each moment of telling is accompanied by a stroke of the chalk (or dry-erase marker, as the case may be). Each stroke, so carefully placed, adds yet another piece to the still-indiscernible puzzle (see figure 1.2, page 44). And the students' delighted squeals are the payoff as the last stroke reveals the all-too-obvious mystery. Students seem to never tire of hearing the episodes again and again. In fact, they, too, are soon repeating the stories as they quickly recall the events mentally. Visit **go.SolutionTree.com/literacy** for a further selection of Chalk Talk examples.

Chalk Talks engage students in *whole-brain activity*, which requires both left-mode and right-mode processing (Sylwester, 1995). The left brain listens and analytically processes the step-by-step, sequential storyline, drawing a logical conclusion based on the evidence presented, while the right brain watches and synthesizes the emerging forms and makes an intuitive leap of insight based on the incomplete patterns. It takes a balance of the verbal and the nonverbal, the logical and the unexpected, the real and the fanciful. As students begin creating their own Chalk Talks, whole-brain processing is present to an even greater degree. Use Chalk Talks in regular classroom curriculum to develop students' listening and visualization skills as well as visual and auditory memory.

Readers of this book can copy the Chalk Talk story from figure 1.2 or one of the other examples available at **go.SolutionTree.com/literacy** if any of them would be appropriate for their students and content. The knowledge-centric focus asks that teachers tap students' prior knowledge about various animals that are most likely familiar to many of the students. For example, students in Florida will jump on the idea of an emerging alligator, while students from Alaska may recognize the bear in the story. This strategy fits perfectly as a read-aloud substitute. Students listen to a story by tuning in to the sound of the language and the visual cues, and students make predictions and inferences—and any customization that works for teachers will still capture the spirit of the activity.

The Butterfly, the Beast, and the Bumblebee

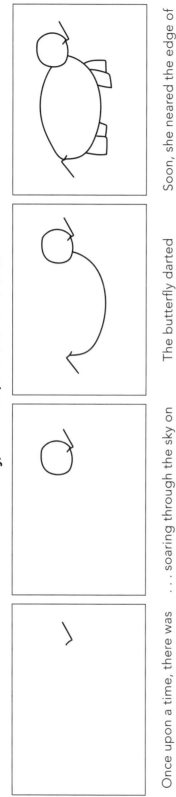

Once upon a time, there was a lovely butterfly . . .

. . . soaring through the sky on a bright, sunlit day.

The butterfly darted about, doing flip-flops and somersaults, enjoying the warmth of the sun.

Soon, she neared the edge of a dense forest . . .

. . . where she met a big, buzzing bumblebee.

The bumblebee buzzed a warning to the butterfly, telling her of the rainy-day beast, who lived quietly in the forest . . . except on rainy days. When the rain came, the beast went wild!

Suddenly, a giant raindrop fell from the sky, and . . .

. . . just as the rainy-day beast appeared, the big, buzzing bumblebee buzzed the butterfly away to safety.

Figure 1.2: Chalk Talk example.

Visit go.SolutionTree.com/literacy for a free reproducible version of this figure.

Session 2: Sound Book

Another activity that Mrs. Clovis uses in her first-grade class to present regular instructional phonics lessons is the Sound Book. The Sound Book itself is a simple stapled and folded paper booklet, but it can represent a foundational part of phonics instruction. This weekly booklet includes daily components to structure phonics schema. Each week, Mrs. Clovis chooses one sound and posts it on the board. The Sound Book activity includes a daily writing component that starts with a tongue twister, a rhyming poem, a jingle, or a saying featuring the chosen sound, which students write down in their weekly Sound Books. This provides students with write-to-read practice that emphasizes the sound, as well as speaking opportunities to use the sound orally in complete sentences when they are reading it (also known as *pictographic reading*; Dehaene, 2009).

In fact, the sound booklets become centerpieces for daily experiences: field trips, painting activity, making a recipe to share, and much more. For example, if Mrs. Clovis chooses the *P* sound, she could use a planned field trip to the pumpkin patch or farm stand to select pumpkins for the class to examine. Or she can simply use a reading assignment about garden-fresh vegetables as a healthy part of the diet to connect to vegetables that start with the *P* sound. Once students have read about pickles, popcorn, and pumpkins, Mrs. Clovis can integrate an activity with mathematics exercises. With the help of supervised fifth graders, the class makes several jack-o-lanterns, gathers the seeds, and dries them. Later, the students count, sort, and line up pumpkin seeds, providing fodder for lots of adding, subtracting, patterns, and pumpkin seed designs to illustrate mathematics words. They can even use the seeds in a recipe-reading session to make a pumpkin seed feast.

Mrs. Clovis uses the Sound Book in parallel with a published reader and a published phonics program. That dual plan ensures that students get a full spectrum of literacy work. The chosen sound of the week provides plenty of ideas for ways to build background knowledge, such as using the letter *P* to expose students to such varied experiences as a real-life farm stand, jack-o-lanterns, and maybe salted pumpkin seed treats. Mrs. Clovis devotes five days to this phonics lesson, with multiple writing, reading, drawing, and speaking activities that immerse students in the *P* sound—and help them distinguish it from other sounds, such as B or D.

Teachers who use the Sound Book strategy will have endless objects to work with as they move through the alphabet. One variation on the Sound Book might have the students identify their favorite food that begins with a special letter of the week. Interestingly, the Sound Book does often seem to relate to something to do with food, recipes, and occasions for a classroom treat or activity of interest, such as a relevant video, story, poem, visit, experience, or even an experiment.

The Sound Book activity can also extend to students' homes. Students can read the various poems, stories, or sentences from their daily writing in their Sound Books and show off their mastery of each sound to parents or caregivers, siblings, pets, or even stuffed animals. They collect signatures from their listeners (a family member can sign for inanimate objects or pets). This weekly ritual is an opportunity to involve students' families in their schoolwork and allow family members to meaningfully participate in their children's learning.

Mrs. Garcia's Fifth-Grade Class

A grades 4–6 lesson on phonics instruction in Mrs. Garcia's fifth-grade class focuses on the reading-writing connection across disciplines.

Session 1: Choral Reading

The Choral Reading activity provides an effective experience of the sound of reading. Usually connected to a curriculum unit, Choral Reading is a marvelous strategy in which students in small groups or pairs read in unison to accentuate the sound of language. Students certainly do appreciate the cleverness and fun of beautifully crafted language or even revealing paragraphs from the biology text or algebra book.

In this instance, Mrs. Garcia has selected the well-known and totally delightful poem by Shel Silverstein (1974), "Sarah Cynthia Sylvia Stout Would Not Take the Garbage Out" (available at https://bit.ly/3hOIk7A), as part of social-emotional learning studies on responsibility. Mrs. Garcia displays the poem on the wall screen, or the student pairs find it on their own screens. She has color-coded lines to designate what the partner As and partner Bs around the room are to read. These can be every other line, paragraph, or page. After an energizing choral reading, partners engage in dialogues to talk about what they have just recited, using the following points (each set of partners selects one point to discuss).

- Determine why the sounds in the poem sound "right."

- Skim and scan the poem for three word choices. The partners choose separately and share their reasons for choosing those words.

- Find one sentence that blows you away because it is so pleasing.

- Score Sarah's sense of responsibility on a scale of 1 to 10 (with 1 being not responsible at all and 10 being totally responsible).

Students often learn essential knowledge from their Choral Reading exercises. In addition to being a wonderful poem for students to have fun with as they read aloud, "Sarah Cynthia Sylvia Stout Would Not Take the Garbage Out" contains a message about taking responsibility. A teacher who uses this strategy could enhance the lesson by emphasizing this social-emotional learning component even more, by putting up reminders on the board near classroom workflow centers that say, "What would Sarah Cynthia Sylvia Stout do?" These would act as reminders to take responsibility to clean up.

Not all teachers will find "Sarah Cynthia Sylvia Stout Would Not Take the Garbage Out" appropriate for their grade level or their content, but many other delightful pieces of writing can accomplish the same goal of helping students improve phonemically by reading aloud challenging, fun passages. For example, in science class, students can learn to read and recite the elements of the periodic table through a fun song that uses the elements as lyrics (see YouTube for versions of these; https://youtu .be/rz4Dd1I_fX0 is a good one). The teacher can print out the lyrics, and students could jigsaw by splitting into groups; each group member takes on a different part of the song and then the group members with those parts gather together to practice their parts before returning to the original groups to say the whole thing (Aronson & Patnoe, 2011). In this way the whole class can get in on the fun. This will challenge fourth- to sixth-grade students, but the challenge is what will engage them.

Session 2: Think-Abouts

While upper-elementary students move from the learning-to-read phase into the reading-to-learn phase, an exercise called Think-Abouts fosters student analyses, comparisons, and elaborations. These texts often feature columns of text, fewer visuals, more complex academic vocabulary, and big, fat fictional chapter books. In this exercise, students learn to define the sounds of *stories* and the sounds of *information* over several class periods. Mrs. Garcia has decided that students will benefit from learning about the concept of purposeful reading and how it plays out when reading both fiction and nonfiction. Using the class's current unit on government as a guide, she selects a traditional, nonfiction document, Abraham Lincoln's Gettysburg Address (UShistory.org, n.d.), and an excerpt from the fictional novel *The Red Badge of Courage* (Crane, 1895).

She instructs student pairs to read aloud both pieces and be aware of *how* they read each one. Then as they talk and compare, she reminds them to note the similarities and differences they discern in terms of initial motivation and interest in the time, events, and character history. In addition, following the task, she directs them to think about their attention, mounting interest, and anything else they recall as they continue their dialogue. She also has them compare how their readings of the documents were alike or different in terms of their vocabulary, fluency, and comprehension, and more important, she has them describe what influence the readings had on them to read more documents like the two class readings. Mrs. Garcia assigns students to write a piece of comparative writing summarizing their experiences as a brief follow-up homework assignment. She closes with a brief talk about the role of purposeful reading in fiction and nonfiction.

Transferring this strategy as a way to compare ideas in the various disciplines is a powerful read-to-learn exercise. The science fiction genre is a natural place to look for passages that explain scientific theories differently but often just as accurately as science textbooks. In fact, the specific subgenre known as *hard science fiction* values scientific accuracy. Hard science fiction weaves technically accurate science into informed speculation, tucking intricate details into the story to back up the writer's extrapolations (Lovely, 2019).

Here is an example of the power of combining fiction and nonfiction reading in a science class from the *New York Times*'s the Learning Network (Fromme, Cutraro, & Schulten, 2012):

> What can you learn about science from fiction? What can you learn about the elements of fiction from stories about the work of real scientists? In this lesson, students learn about the genre of "lab lit," then choose from a number of activities to explore an area of science through reading and writing lab lit.

For this activity, teachers should divide students into pairs and have the partners each read one of the following two excerpts alone and then read their excerpt aloud to their partner. This way, both students have an opportunity for silent reading and for reading to an audience.

1. Two paragraphs from *Spillover: Animal Infections and the Next Human Pandemic* by David Quammen (2012), beginning with "By the time Reid rushed back to the stables, she was dead" on page 15

2. Two pages from *Intuition* by Allegra Goodman (2006), beginning with "Cliff's cheeks were burning" on page 5

Teachers should then ask student pairs to discuss whether they think the passages are fact or fiction and why. And teachers should have the pairs decide which passage does a better job of explaining the science that is the subject of the excerpt (Fromme et al., 2012).

Mr. Perkins's Eighth-Grade Mathematics Class

In the middle school years, students concentrate on subtle and sophisticated sounds in tone and tenor, pacing, pauses, full stops, and exclamations; they are looking for patterns, understanding, and interpretation. Mr. Perkins uses a strategy called Tear Share to have students solve, show, and tell in a cooperative way. While mathematics class is not always known for its literacy exercises, Mr. Perkins's lesson on the language of mathematics is knowledge driven. It encourages students to use reading and writing to solve a problem based on reasoning, rather than sticking to computational mathematical exercises.

To begin, he groups students into fours with their chairs in a compass configuration—that is, north is 1, south is 2, east is 3, and west is 4. He has students each fold a single sheet of paper in half and in half again to make four square sections. Then they unfold it and label each corner 1, 2, 3, and 4 and copy four prompts in the spaces (see figure 1.3).

1. Solve	2. Show
If the day before the day before yesterday was Monday, what is the day after the day after tomorrow?	Use drawings, graphics, and pictures to show how you reached your response to prompt 1.
3. Tell	4. Share
Explain in writing your reasoning and how you arrived at your final conclusion. Include reasons why your process was an easy way to solve the problem.	Describe in writing how this problem is different from or the same as the mathematics problems you are usually asked to do.

Figure 1.3: Tear Share example.

Once their sheets of paper are ready, Mr. Perkins directs his students to do the following.

1. Respond to all four prompts on their own in the four to five minutes of allotted time.

2. Tear their papers into four sections and pass the sections to the corresponding numbers of each partner. That is, student 1 receives all the answers to prompt 1, student 2 receives all the answers to prompt 2, and so on.

3. Read the four responses that have the exact same number they have collected and prepare an oral summary.

4. In three minutes, take turns sharing their oral summaries within their group of four. Mr. Perkins monitors the groups and then moves on.

5. Mr. Perkins gets everyone's attention and samples several oral summaries by asking different groups to share their conclusions.

Because the content presented in the Tear Share strategy is so specific, it stands to reason that most teachers will customize it so that it fits their students and their content. A customized variation in a mathematics class could entail putting a relevant equation on the board instead of on paper. The students then solve the equation and put their answers in corner number 1 before continuing as described.

An ELA teacher could have all students read a page from a story that they are familiar with, meaning they will be better prepared. Then they perform a Tear Share with the following prompts.

1. Briefly *infer* what might have happened in this story before this excerpt.

2. *Predict* what could happen next.

3. *Identify* one of the elements of the story (such as character, setting, or plot).

4. *Write* a five-word surprise closing to their comment.

Dr. Hamilton's Grades 10–12 Humanities 101 Elective

Secondary (grades 9–12) students are expected to exercise sophisticated phonics skills across literacy fields, including evidence-based analysis. Dr. Hamilton achieves this through an activity called Triangle Read.

In his Humanities 101 class, Dr. Hamilton often combines literature and history as the jumping-off point for small-group classroom discourse to afford students opportunities for speaking with authority on evidence-based text passages. For example, Dr. Hamilton's students analyze primary sources in an effort to answer the central historical question, "What sank the *USS Maine*?" He challenges the students to determine which contemporary New York City newspaper was a more reliable source of information: the *New York Herald* or the *New York Times*.

Dr. Hamilton introduces them to the topic and provides one article from each newspaper about the sinking of the *USS Maine* in Havana Harbor in February 1898. Both sources of information have their own bias. Students in groups of three read the two articles aloud; then, as a group, they annotate or highlight what they all agree are key differences in the documents.

The students each generate and write down at least three higher-order questions (Bloom, 1956; Webb, 1999) and share them with their group members. Then the groups pick two questions out of the nine they have generated to use in a whole-class discussion. They make their choices based on the amount of evidence they can show, what makes the most sense, and how prepared they feel about their choices.

Classroom examples at this grade level are always very content specific simply because content is what students are learning in high school. For this reason, the metacognitive reflection about the evidence, the process, and the pros and cons of the activity will focus on how teachers must customize this lesson for their own content. One other possibility to enhance the rigor of the assignment is to do the strategy just as it is described in Dr. Hamilton's class but using contrasting news broadcasts from two different cable TV news channels as the source material. This would apply to a lesson primarily about media bias, propaganda, and sensationalism.

Having each student generate three higher-level questions before sharing them with their team members is a feature of the strategy that teachers can apply in multiple ways, as it is a good way to teach students to generate good questions while they are reading. This simple skill reinforces the idea that silent reading is a conversation that happens in readers' minds, between themselves and the author. So, when students receive a reading assignment, instead of answering questions, they have to generate their own higher-level questions.

One creative way to transfer this strategy is to have students anonymously post their questions on the class website after they have done their reading as homework. Their classmates can then rank the questions for originality and effectiveness using a student-safe social media tool such as Poll Everywhere (www.polleverywhere.com), where names are anonymous. This simple innovation becomes a great way for the students to generate, read, and evaluate multiple questions on the topic being taught.

PLC Discussion Questions

We provide these discussion questions for use within department or grade-level teams. If your school functions as a professional learning community, these questions are an effective way to encourage professional dialogue in your collaborative team. Conversations like this are key to building trust within the team and helping team members learn from one another. Choose one or several based on interest and concerns exposed during a book study or independent reading of this book.

- Many state and federal policies around phonics instruction call for it to be systematic and explicit. Explain to what extent you feel your phonics approach is systematic and explicit.

- Do you agree or disagree that all students and aspiring readers benefit from learning phonics first? Why?

- Individually generate and rank five facts about the importance of reading aloud to students, and then as a team, share and compare the results of your analysis. What conclusions can you draw based on your discussion?

- What would be the easiest and quickest way to begin reading more to your students in every grade and every subject?

- What evidence from your own classroom or independent research could you offer that supports the assertation that around the grade 8 level, the listening level of a student (the level at which he or she hears and comprehends text) is significantly higher than his or her silent reading level?

- If being read aloud to were a significant part of your students' instructional day, what effect do you think it would have on their social-emotional learning?

- What are some things your school is doing to increase equity in literacy acquisition among students of different backgrounds?

Resources for Learning More

A comprehensive summary of research on phonics is available from the Education Endowment Foundation (n.d.; https://bit.ly/2TNzHzE). You may wish to review this summary and pay particular attention to the What Should I Consider? section.

Anne Castles, Kathleen Rastle, and Kate Nation's (2018) article titled "Ending the Reading Wars: Reading Acquisition From Novice to Expert" is an excellent piece that provides greater detail on this topic. Visit https://bit.ly/2ZNELIu to read the article online.

For a deep dive into precisely what the body of evidence around phonics instruction says and does not say, check out Jeffrey S. Bowers's (2020) article "Reconsidering the Evidence That Systematic Phonics Is More Effective Than Alternative Methods of Reading Instruction" in *Educational Psychology Review* (https://bit.ly/2Ak12Te).

CHAPTER 2

The Look of Reading—Vocabulary

I love the book and the look of words
the weight of ideas that popped into my mind
I love the tracks
of new thinking in my mind.

—Maya Angelou

Mrs. Wayman believes that we often choose a book by its looks, the cover and graphics, or the title, so she likes to take her eighth-grade English class to the school media center. She instructs students, "Look around the shelves for books that catch your eye—books that make you stop for a closer look at them. Then pull one book from the shelf, turn it over, open it, and read a paragraph." Again, Mrs. Wayman's experience has shown her that even during the first look inside the book, before you've read a word, you can see with your eyes the solid page of smallish text or the graphics that invite more exploration. She wants her students to be aware of the visceral sense that books bring out in us in our choices. She then says, "Decide if it is the one you want to read independently. Be ready to describe what tempted you to pick that one book. What were you looking at that interested you?" Her goal is to always have students understand why they do what they do, in this case, in choosing a book. And finally, she closes with a highly insightful task: "See if you can generalize the reading choices you look at for your independent reading."

Exposure to voice and choice and the ability to make personal decisions regarding reading and writing options invite students into the world of literacy. Reflecting on the experience anchors those feelings for the students.

Students see evidence of language everywhere, with printed words appearing on signage, screens, chalkboards, and much more; they see words, words, and more words throughout the school building and in K–12 classrooms. Not only is it a world of sounds galore, but it is also a world of letters, words, images, and graphics galore. Thus, with that overture, let's explore this fascinating element called the *look of reading*. It's different from the sound of reading, but altogether compatible with the picture of fluent literacy.

The String of Things

An image that rings true regarding the look of reading is to see language as a string of things. In fact, this provides a vivid way to view how language comes together. Theoretical physicist Brian Greene (2012) offers a comparison that makes lots of sense:

> The central idea of string theory is quite straightforward. It says that if you examine any piece of matter ever more finely, at first, you'll find molecules and then you'll find atoms and subatomic particles. . . . If you could probe smaller, much smaller than we can with existing energy, you'd find something else inside these particles— a little tiny vibrating filament of energy, a little tiny vibrating string.

Willingham (2017) suggests the string of things in language might look like this: letters, words, phrases, sentences, paragraphs, pages, content, chapters, books. To many readers grounded in the look of written words, sentences, paragraphs, and so on, this presents a viable picture of reading matter.

- **The look of a letter:** Straight shape, curved shape, cursive, font, size, italics, bold, capitalization

- **The look of a word:** Short word, long word, antonym, synonym, homonym

- **The look of a phrase:** Fragment, thought, no punctuation, unfinished idea

- **The look of a sentence:** Simple, compound, complex, long, short, average

- **The look of a question:** Academic, universal, essential, silly, ludicrous

- **The look of a purpose:** Explanation, description, argument, persuasion

- **The look of an exclamation:** One word, an entire cheer, surprise, disbelief

- **The look of a paragraph:** Indentation, long, short, dialogue, break, punctuation

- **The look of a page of content:** Text, fonts, images, columns, figures, page number
- **The look of a chapter:** Title, story, paragraphs, footnotes, citations, opening and ending pages
- **The look of a book:** Hardcover, paperback, digital device, title, author, table of contents, bibliography

On a humorous note, the protagonist of the Charles Dickens (1861/1973) novel *Great Expectations*, Pip, notes, "I struggled through the alphabet as if it had been a bramble-bush; getting considerably worried and scratched by every letter" (p. 92). This delightful quote seems to mirror the feelings of many young readers as they struggle through the reading as if it were that same bramble bush.

Willingham (2017) shows that the beautiful metaphor of a string of things illustrates how the reader and writer string words together to create thoughts on paper or on a screen. The magic of this process is that reading, writing, speaking, and listening are all rather linear yet quite connected to each other at the same time. In fact, the concept of the string of things in terms of speaking, listening, reading, and writing illustrates the line of progress we follow becoming literate people. As they say, one step at a time.

The look of reading starts with the spoken language of preK–3 learners, which includes common nouns like *mom, dad, sister, house, car, tree,* and *street,* and small-talk words like *yes, no, thank you, start, stop, yes,* and *not now.* From there, these early learners quickly become capable with functional verbs like *laugh, walk, tell, climb, throw, jump,* and *clap.*

As intermediate learners progress in their literacy work of reading, writing, speaking, and listening, they move well beyond those everyday words, and their vocabulary expands widely, just as their world does. Middle schoolers are well into textbook work, and they read on every kind of electronic device. They are seasoned gamers, so the look of literacy is high in imagery and animation, with constantly changing innovations that keep them engrossed in the user experience. And their academic literacy skills develop and mature, in spite of the distractions of the electronic playthings. In fact, from the middle teens to the secondary and postgraduate years, digital reading and writing are fast taking over the helm of literacy as we knew it. We'll highlight this shift in chapter 4 (page 131).

Reading: The Brain's Letterbox

As previously mentioned, human beings are born prewired to understand spoken language—the sound of language. But this chapter transitions to an area where we humans have no physiological predisposition—the look of reading. While we naturally absorb spoken language, Dehaene (2009) observes, "Nothing in our evolution could have prepared us to absorb language through vision" (p. 4). Reading, therefore, is a rather unnatural act that requires instruction and some physiological changes to our brains that can only occur through practice.

French cognitive neuroscientist Stanislas Dehaene (2009) has led the work in this area of study, which he profiles in his highly regarded book *Reading in the Brain: The New Science of How We Read*. His "firm conviction is that every teacher should have some notion of how reading operates in the child's brain" (Dehaene, 2009, p. 232). He laments, however, that since most educators are not exposed to cognitive science during preservice coursework or book studies, it is often the case that "teachers know more about the working of their car" than their students' brains (WISE Channel, 2013).

Dehaene's (2009) work focuses on an area of the brain that he refers to as the *brain's letterbox*, where physiological changes occur in direct relation to literacy acquisition. Essentially, this area in our brains becomes repurposed, thereby connecting previously unconnected areas related to visual inputs, sound, and meaning. This allows us to associate visual inputs (letters and words) with already-connected sounds and meanings—to read.

Dehaene (2009) refers to the changes our brains go through as a result of reading instruction as *neuronal recycling* because "when we learn a new skill, we recycle some of our old primate brain circuits" (p. 7). While some social scientists previously envisioned the brain "as an infinitely plastic organ whose learning capacity [was] so broad that it [placed] no constraints on the scope of human activity," he and his colleagues assert that the brain is actually a very "structured device that manages to convert some of its parts to a new use" (Dehaene, 2009, pp. 6–7). In this case, we repurpose a section of our primate brain that once supported us with highly visual activities—likely things such as reading minute signs of prey in fields and forests and remembering faces—to allow us to take in letters and, through training, associate them with sounds and meanings.

Once we understand the profundity of physiological changes wrought by literacy, we can view reading as nothing less than remarkable. After the appropriate training and experiences, "any reader easily retrieves a single meaning out of at least 50,000 candidate words, in the space of a few tenths of a second, based on a few strokes of light on the retina" (Dehaene, 2009, p. 42).

To be more precise, capable readers recognize and take in the meaning of known words in just fifty milliseconds, or 0.05 seconds (Dehaene, 2009). This results in a dynamic where, accounting for the time needed for the eye to move across a page, most good readers "read from four hundred to five hundred words per minute" (Dehaene, 2009, p. 17). Dehaene (2009) reminds us, as good readers, "it's only because these processes have become automatic and unconscious, thanks to years of practice, that we are under the *illusion* that reading is simple and effortless" (p. 8, emphasis added).

For students just beginning literacy instruction, "the spelling-sound translation process is laborious" (Willingham, 2017, p. 56). As Castles et al. (2018) note, "To become confident, successful readers, children need to learn to recognize words and compute their meanings rapidly without having to engage in translation back to sounds" (p. 2). They need what cognitive scientists call *orthographic representations*, the ability to recognize words instantly. These can only develop through practice.

When students practice reading enough, they become able to self-teach, initiating a cycle of learning that fuels lifelong reading. We'll cover this fascinating process in the following sections.

Learning to Read Enables Self-Teaching

Let's revisit the model of reading acquisition advanced by Uta Frith (1985), as this model will now provide additional context for our present discussion (as cited in Dehaene, 2009). The model begins with the previously discussed pictorial or logographic stage, when students do not truly master reading but look at words exactly as they do objects or faces. They read by recognizing the whole, and their reading is limited to a small set of very familiar words that they have come to know purely through repeated exposure (for example, their name or a familiar logo). However, the same student who recognizes the scripted Coca-Cola logo would likely not be able to read *Coca-Cola* in a different font, and certainly not *COcA-colA* (see figure 2.1). In this sense, what students are doing in this phase, though sometimes called "reading," actually has little association with what truly advanced readers do. These students are, in a sense, recognizing pictures.

Figure 2.1: Coca-Cola letters in different fonts.

The next stage is the phonological stage, which is typified by the development of a grapheme-to-phoneme conversion procedure (Frith, 1985, as cited in Dehaene, 2009). This is what teachers must teach, and it begins a transition where, instead of seeing words as a whole (for example, knowing or not knowing *Coca-Cola* written one way), students can now sound out unknown words. From a Dehaene-based perspective, they are beginning to rework their brains through neuronal recycling to form the letterbox. Visual inputs (letter symbols) are being associated with sound and meaning. Reading, in a truer sense, is beginning.

In the final stage, the orthographic stage, things become quite formal, and readers become able to take in visual representations of words (regardless of font, type style, or case) and associate them with sounds and meaning in milliseconds (Frith, 1985, as cited in Dehaene, 2009). They have developed strong orthographic representations and are mastering "the look of reading." We should note that Frith's stages are "not rigidly partitioned," meaning that students can be fully in the orthographic stage for certain letter combinations and sounds while still in the phonological stage with others (Dehaene, 2009, p. 199).

The impact of a growing collection of orthographic representations is significant:

> As he gains reading experience, the child develops a larger and larger repertoire of words he can recognize at a glance, rather than sounding out. And the representations of individual words (and letter groups) get stronger, and more reliable. As this happens, the child's reading becomes faster, smoother, and more accurate. (Willingham, 2017, p. 66)

At this point, reading comprehension increases substantially because "adding orthographic representations results in a smaller attention demand for decoding, leaving more attention available for comprehending what you're reading" (Willingham, 2017, p. 72). This, in turn, facilitates students' reading development: "Children make the transition from being 'novices,' reading words primarily via alphabetic decoding, to 'experts,' recognizing familiar written words rapidly and automatically, mapping their spellings directly to their meanings without recourse to decoding" (Castles et al., 2018, p. 19). Then, after enough exposure to language, something rather remarkable begins to occur: students begin a process of self-teaching.

Share (1999) frames the acquisition of orthographic representations as self-teaching. He advises that "the self-teaching hypothesis argues that the process of word recognition will depend primarily on the frequency to which a [reader] has been exposed to a particular word" (Share, 1995, p. 155). In other words, has the reader seen the word enough times that he or she has developed the ability to recognize it in milliseconds?

Share (1999) also notes that self-teaching occurs "not merely for the beginner, but throughout the entire ability range" (p. 97). We are constantly taking in new words through repeated exposure. As Castles et al. (2018) assert regarding fluent word-recognition skills, "experience matters" (p. 8). There is no magical or mysterious aspect to acquiring orthographic representations. It is about practicing reading by engaging with text—lots of text.

When we already know a word from having heard and perhaps even spoken it, self-teaching is very straightforward. We sound out the word that we initially perceive as unknown only to find that, in many ways, it is known to us. We just do not have a sufficient orthographic representation. A student, for example, might have heard the word *facade* but expected it to begin with *ph-* or have included an *s*. When the student first encounters *facade* in print, he or she does not immediately recognize it. Upon sounding out the word, however, the student recognizes its meaning, and the process of building an orthographic representation for it begins. Once we have seen individual words enough times, we build strong orthographic representations.

But what about words we may have never heard before? It turns out that it is possible for us to teach ourselves unknown words, or at least figure out a good portion of their meanings in many cases.

To understand how this type of self-teaching is possible, the concept of *morphemes*—"the smallest units that carry some meaning"—is relevant (Dehaene, 2009, p. 22). For example, we may know that words that end with *-ed* are generally in the past tense, and a word that begins with *pre-* implies something that happens before or is a condition. After appropriate phonetic instruction and practice with written language, we become capable of reading, not through memorizing whole words but primarily through breaking down words into their corresponding morphemes and letter blends. This is when our self-teaching goes to a much higher level, as "breaking down a word into its morphemes [can often allow] us to understand words that we have never seen before" (Dehaene, 2009, p. 22).

Consider the words *reunbutton* and *deglochization*; one we fully understand, and the other we understand is "the undoing of the action of 'gloching,' whatever that may be" (Dehaene, 2009, p. 22). Earlier in this book, we employed a novel word: *overskillification*. You knew the morphemes, the smallest letter pairings with meanings. No additional explanation was required.

The potential of self-teaching, particularly when encountering unknown words, is a major consideration within literacy acquisition. When we see an unknown word, we employ a process called *phonological recoding*—using our knowledge of the relationships between letters and phonemes to figure out pronunciation. Share (1999) remarks, "Because so very many words occur so very rarely in print, the self-teaching opportunities afforded by phonological recoding may well represent the 'cutting edge' of reading development" (p. 97). Teachers can have students growing on the cutting edge if and only if they understand and create the conditions necessary for self-teaching. Dehaene (2009) hints at the necessary conditions when he notes, "The expert reader is, above all, a *well-read* man or woman who implicitly knows a large number of prefixes, roots, and suffixes and effortlessly associates them with pronunciation and meaning" (p. 204, emphasis added). This mirrors a refrain that we have come to before: becoming highly literate requires exposure to and engagement with lots of text.

Engage in Massive Amounts of Reading and Writing

Massive amounts of reading may seem overwhelming, but we use this term intentionally to emphasize the salient point that expert voices mentioned throughout the text are making. Now that we understand and appreciate the capacity of self-teaching, the implications are clear: "Once students can effectively decode, we must organize time in language arts to ensure that students spend large amounts of time reading, both purposefully and for pleasure" (Schmoker, 2018, p. 132). As researchers Keith E. Stanovich and Richard F. West (1989) state, "The single most effective pathway to fluent word reading is print experience: Children need to see as many words as possible, as frequently as possible" (as cited in Castles et al., 2018, p. 26). Schmoker (2018) advises, "Once students learn to decode, they learn to read better and acquire large amounts of vocabulary and content knowledge by reading—not by enduring more skills instruction" (p. 131).

Could it be that simple? Could it be that many of our students who struggle do so primarily because they simply do not practice the activity of reading enough? We all often feel that the answer to such a significant problem could not possibly be that easy, yet many data points would suggest that it is. Willingham (2017) notes that while "reluctant readers read 50,000 words each year, . . . avid readers encounter many more words—as many as 4,000,000" (p. 68). Quite similarly, teaching software developer Terry Paul (1992) finds that the "top 5% of readers read 144 times more than the bottom 5%" (p. 7). Engagement with text during the school years varies widely, as does critical exposure to oral language prior to school (Gilkerson et al., 2017; Hart & Risley, 1995). This all creates a dynamic wherein some students flourish in print-rich environments, while others languish in print-impoverished ones or choose not to engage with texts that are afforded to them.

Creating fertile conditions where all students are immersed in and deeply engage with print should be our primary objective, yet Schmoker (2018) believes that "literacy-rich curriculum is exceedingly rare in our schools" (p. 24) and that, if you were to walk into any language arts classroom, the two things you would most likely *not* see students doing are reading and writing. In class, our focus can too often fall on activities other than reading and writing, and few students read substantially outside of class.

This would explain why there are so many garden-variety struggling (GVS) readers. They have the necessary abilities. We have even taught them to decode sufficiently. But they fail to flourish because they don't get the opportunity to regularly and adequately practice the essential activities of literacy, including vocabulary building, fluency, and comprehension, by engaging in massive amounts of reading and writing. According to student surveys from NAEP participants, 61 percent of seventeen-year-olds report reading "less than once a week" or "never or hardly ever." This is up substantially from only 36 percent in 1984 (National Center for Education Statistics, n.d.).

Focus on the Most Important Standard of All

Schmoker (2011) remarks that, paradoxically, "current reading and language arts standards interfere with the acquisition of literacy" (p. 101). He and other authors contend we are so focused on teaching the skills of reading that we leave little room for students to participate in authentic literacy activities—reading, writing, speaking, and listening. Schmoker (2011) refers to many language arts standards documents as "trivial" because they "do very little to clarify the amount of reading and writing students must do to become truly literate—which may be *the most important 'standard' of all*" (p. 112). He asserts that "very early on, there is a place for phonics, phonemic units, and certain reading skills" but questions whether "we are guilty of overkill" (Schmoker, 2011, p. 102).

To address the perceived deficiency in language arts standards documents, Schmoker (2011) recommends that once students are capable of reading and writing independently, "for every English course [or grade level]. . . teams establish standards that approximate" (p. 116) the following amount of required instructional reading for all students at all grade levels.

- About ten to fifteen books and plays, depending on their length and density

- Multiple poems and short stories (perhaps ten to fifteen of each)

- Between twenty and forty newspaper, magazine, or online articles

These should be divided sensibly among the following categories.

- Fiction (imaginative literature and poetry—about 40–60 percent)

- Nonfiction and literary nonfiction (biographies, memoirs, and true stories—about 40–50 percent, of which 25–40 percent can be self-selected)

We recognize that this is a lot of reading. That's the point! In the next section we'll discuss how to vary the kinds of reading teachers can expect students to do using three different best practices: (1) reading to students, (2) having students read independently, and (3) reading with other students.

Methods: How Students Can Do All This Reading

Before we proceed any further, we must divide discussions about reading into a few distinctly different categories—reading *to* students, having students *read independently*, and *reading with* students (instructional reading). This is critically important, as different rules govern what constitutes success within each category, and how we handle them profoundly impacts the vocabulary acquisition of students.

An example of how these three categories of reading are distinct relates to the choice of texts. The Common Core State Standards, for example, have very specific recommendations for instructional reading, which it refers to as *text complexity grade bands* (NGA & CCSSO, 2010). Also, with instructional reading, we want students to think deeply and analytically and respond, most likely in writing, to open-ended, text-based questions. However, when students are reading independently for pleasure, we can afford to be a bit less concerned about text complexity; reading text on the far edge or even above grade level would be overly taxing. And if we required students to write a paper about every book they read for pleasure, the pleasure would likely soon fade away. The following sections explore each category of reading in further detail and include a brief review of our conclusions about the value of reading to students.

Read to Students

As noted previously, evidence shows that reading to students of all ages and all levels, in all disciplines and subjects, in all forms, and as often as possible is a uniquely powerful technique for reinforcing reading fluency and student comprehension. When students have an opportunity to hear the technical reading of a science passage, for example, they receive many benefits, from the correct pronunciation of certain words, the proper patterning of a particular scientific concept, and the sense of wholeness inherent in hearing an expressive and comprehensive piece read to them in an effortless stream of language. All these bring a fresh understanding and more robust comprehension. In addition, it's appropriate to read material that's two grade levels above students' current level. This helps them capture the sound of words, make more connections to prior knowledge as they have time to digest it, and boost their own reading of at-grade-level material.

Reading aloud to students provides opportunities to hear a substantive piece of reading, uninterrupted, with a fluency that facilitates deeper processing. We have found that this simple strategy builds students' confidence and increases their self-esteem as they witness the teacher modeling the reading.

When it's time for students to read independently, the model the teacher has provided is very helpful; students will follow that model in turn when they read the same passage. Let's now explore the power of students' reading independently.

Have Students Read Independently

For years, academics and educators have known the highly documented relationship between wide independent reading and academic success, yet we have ignored its profundity and implications. Figure 2.2 depicts a profound insight about the *minimum* amount of independent reading time students need to be successful. Decades of data collected by Renaissance Learning (2015) repeatedly reveal that U.S. students who

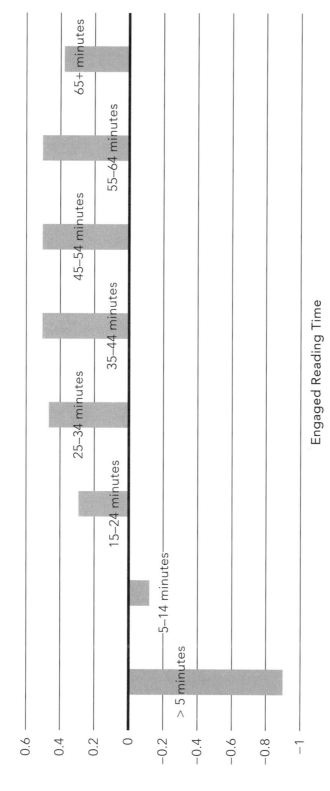

Source: Renaissance Learning, 2015.

Figure 2.2: Normal curve equivalent gain in relation to daily reading.

read less than fifteen minutes a day consistently fail to keep up with rising expectations, while students who read more than fifteen minutes a day consistently progress at or above national norms. The metric shows the normal curve equivalent (NCE) score. It's important to note that when NCEs are positive, growth is occurring. When they are negative, student learning is declining.

Sadly, its analysis also reveals that more than half of U.S. students fail to read fifteen minutes a day (Renaissance Learning, 2015). Taken together, these two findings clearly suggest that more than half of U.S. students are simply not reading enough to keep up with rising expectations.

For our purposes, *independent reading* means reading that students do for pleasure with a substantial degree of choice. In some studies, independent reading seems to include any reading that students do without the teacher. This might include anything from expressly assigned specific texts, a chapter from a novel the class is reading together for instructional purposes, or when the teacher says, "Finish this section tonight at home." We contend that assigned readings and portions of texts assigned for instructional reading that students finish are merely extensions of instructional reading, despite the fact that the reading occurs independently.

We also contend that wide independent reading holds significant, overlooked, and undervalued potential. This essential activity uniquely fosters the self-teaching necessary to become highly literate. At first, it helps elementary students learn the letter combinations of English and immediately recognize more words by sight, but then in the intermediate grades, it transitions into an activity that helps readers of all ages develop vocabulary and other critical elements of literacy, such as facility with advanced literacy decisions like word choice, parallel structure, logical thinking, and grammar rules. These benefits continue for the rest of their lives and contribute to literacy excellence.

Schools seeking to foster rich independent reading have a variety of options. Less formal programs such as Drop Everything and Read (DEAR), free uninterrupted reading (FUR), and numerous iterations of sustained silent reading (SSR) abound, as do more formal and structured approaches such as Accelerated Reader (www.renaissance.com/products/accelerated-reader) and myON Reader (www.myon.com).

Regardless of which program or approach a school uses, Lemov et al. (2016) encourage teachers to implement accountable independent reading. The challenge, they say, is that "it's hard to be completely sure whether [students] are actually reading. Or whether they are practicing effective habits or inscribing poor ones" (Lemov et al., 2016, p. 218). Teachers should include some form of accountability and monitoring of comprehension, such as a three-minute miniconference between the teacher and the student when a book is completed, a short comprehension quiz, or a brief ad developed by the student to promote the book on the designated spaces on a classroom bulletin board. Without measures like these, independent reading can have the unintended consequence of "functioning regressively—that is, as an activity that causes good readers to get better by practicing effective habits, and bad readers to get worse by reinforcing bad habits" (Lemov et al., 2016, p. 218).

Lemov et al.'s (2016) ideas line up with those of education and social research professor Keith J. Topping, who has widely reviewed the research on less formal independent reading programs compared to structured programs like Accelerated Reader. He finds that "the practice of allocating sustained silent reading (SSR) time in schools noted mixed results, with six studies finding a positive effect on reading scores and five no effect" (Topping, Samuels, & Paul, 2007, p. 191) while "data suggested that student reading ability was strongly positive related to amount of in-school reading practice [with Accelerated Reader data]" (Topping & Paul, 2011). He asserts that "'reading practice' is not a homogeneous, unitary activity; the quality and effectiveness of that practice also require consideration" and the monitoring of these elements is more easily achieved with more structured programs (Topping, 2001, p. 156).

Paul (2003) echoes this sentiment as well as Lemov et al.'s (2016) concerns about unmonitored independent reading practice functioning regressively when he notes that "letting students 'just read' on their own can, in some situations, actually lower reading achievement relative to their peers" and that "unguided independent reading is not supported [by research], particularly for low-achieving students" (p. 2). Lemov et al. (2016) emphasize quality over quantity with independent reading. Decades of data collected by Renaissance Learning (2015) support that recommendation and as the authors alluded to earlier, the more students read, the more fluent and knowledgeable they become at literacy excellence.

Paul (2003) notes, "Teachers and students [can] focus on three goals for independent reading practice: quality, quantity, and challenge" (p. 8). While elements of all three of these are associated with growth, "of the three, quality has consistently been found to be most critical in ensuring that reading practice will lead to improvements in reading ability," and "the next most important factor is quantity" (Paul, 2003, p. 8). While the concept of massive amounts of reading is one of our major themes, we stress both accountability within that activity and a purposeful emphasis on the quality of reading over the quantity. The final factor, the challenge level of a book, proves more complex, partially due to variability in readability formulas and student motivation (Paul, 2003). Paul's (2003) analysis finds that "students can read a very broad range of books, both easy and difficult, and still have successful reading experiences and achieve significant gains in reading," causing him to ultimately conclude that, instead of focusing on book level as a hard and firm indicator, "teachers can and should allow students a fair amount of freedom to choose their books and follow their interests" (p. 43) during independent reading.

Despite the documented power of independent reading, some schools question devoting time for daily independent reading practice, pushing back and asking the pejorative question, "How could we possibly schedule that much time for students to be 'just reading'?" Secondary schools in particular are wary of the time commitment, as they hold the belief that their students do not need this practice time because they already know how to read. Yet, as we have seen, when students engage is less than fifteen minutes of daily reading practice, they are consistently unable to keep up with rising levels of expectation.

Daily reading practice is not time spent "just reading." It's self-teaching time, and it must occur across all grade levels. Much more goes on during this activity than we may have realized before. When engaging in independent reading time, students are managing their own learning and become more capable of self-agency.

Read With Students

Having now explored both reading to students and independent reading by students, we are left with one final category: instructional reading. In fact, it might be most appropriate to refer to this category as *reading with students* because, during most of this type of reading practice, the teacher is ever present. The teacher is reviewing necessary background information during prereading or activating knowledge that students already possess during an *anticipatory set*, which is material the teacher may use to prepare students by stirring up prior knowledge. Reading teachers call out words and details, pose questions, evoke conversations, and model *think-alouds*, which is a technique of talking students through what the teacher is thinking about as he or she reads a piece. In contrast with the extended periods of uninterrupted flow that occur when reading to students or during dedicated independent reading time, reading with students is often punctuated with all sorts of activities.

Reading with students should be a significant portion of class time; 25 percent of the period should be teacher led. Guided literacy exercises are complex and often involve new material, meaning that students benefit from a teacher-supervised discussion. Here is where concerns about the complexity of text are more warranted, and where discussions and written responses to higher-level, open-ended questions are not only useful but mandatory. These types of questions are key to deeper thinking about the text. That said, as previously noted, we should be cautious about the dangers of overskillification.

Table 2.1 summarizes the three reading categories and the rules that govern them.

Table 2.1: Three Categories of Student Reading

Category of Student Reading	Guidance for Teachers
Reading to Students (Instructional Oral Language)	For optimum growth, teachers should choose reading materials written at roughly two grade levels above students' current reading level.
Having Students Read by Themselves (Completely Independent Practice)	Both MetaMetrics (with its Lexile measures; www.lexile.com) and Renaissance Learning (www.renaissance.com) have suggestions for appropriate independent reading ranges. To ensure success, it is also important that teachers monitor for sufficient comprehension.
Reading With Students (Instructional Strategic Guidance)	Here, our ELA curriculum and core texts take a central role. The Common Core's text-complexity grade bands and other guidance for what constitutes grade-level text are critical. Teachers commonly use complex text; universal, open-ended questions; close reading; expert guidance; and writing in response to text as central, recurring activities.

Each form of reading offers unique benefits. We read *to students* to expose them to new vocabulary, syntax, pacing, and expression by tapping into the fact that humans are prewired to learn language by hearing it spoken. We read *with students* for the bulk of our instructional activities to ask them to perform on the edge of their abilities and in deep, critical, and reflective ways. Finally, we create time for students to read *independently* so they can do the critical self-teaching that can only occur in that way.

Each of these activities distinctively contributes to vocabulary acquisition, an absolutely critical part of the big three. In fact, without vast vocabulary development, content knowledge suffers greatly. Remember, words play a vital role in concept development across the disciplines. Words, vocabulary, and meaning are inextricably linked to knowledge and knowingness. In the journey of literacy, phonics has a premier role at the beginning, which lessens as the journey goes on. Vocabulary takes over that role next.

Vocabulary: The Building Blocks of Conceptual Knowledge

As humans, we see the world in words and interact with them vicariously. We see the staunch and steady words on a printed page, and we see, too, text staring at us from a brightly lit screen with instantly changeable fonts, styles, and sizes. And we proceed to read or to slip back and double down on a particular phrase still on our mind.

Vocabulary—and, for that matter, the entire world of words, word forms, word families, and the meanings they represent—shapes the concepts of our personal knowledge base. Beginning with a bare-bones vocabulary of known words, the mind quickly grasps a working vocabulary from its experiences and interactions with language. The look of literacy encompasses the images of words that, in turn, create developing concepts. These emerge as patterns that connect and form the critical pathways of deep understanding.

Words don't stand in isolation; they represent entire concepts. That's why they matter so much in knowledge acquisition: "The central moment in concept formation, and its generative cause, is a specific use of words as functional 'tools'" (Vygotsky, 1986, p. 107). Before we discuss how to help students better acquire vocabulary, it would serve us well to review how crucial vocabulary knowledge is to comprehension.

> *Words don't stand in isolation; they represent entire concepts. That's why they matter so much in knowledge acquisition: "The central moment in concept formation, and its generative cause, is a specific use of words as functional 'tools'" (Vygotsky, 1986, p. 107).*

Vocabulary acquisition reigns supreme above all elements of literacy as a craft. We can safely assume that voracious readers have an enormous vocabulary. The more one reads, the bigger one's vocabulary. And the bigger one's vocabulary, the easier the path to reading success, which naturally leads to more reading. Why? Because people like to do what they're good at doing. Thus, in our experience, good readers are self-driven to read as often as they can.

On the other hand, hesitant, stop-and-start readers who experience interruptions in the flow of the words and fluency needed for comprehension more often than not become discouraged readers who frequently avoid reading as their way to get information. Rather, they develop robust schemata of prior knowledge and connectivity from listening to others talk about the meaning, and somehow glean as much as they need to achieve a low level of understanding.

As previously noted, we humans have a low tolerance for unknown words in the texts we read. We need to know approximately *98 percent* or more of the words to find meaning (Willingham, 2017). To experience this, take a look at the passage in figure 2.3, which uses blank spaces to represent words you, the reader, do not know.

_____

All the _____ _____ around, or _____,
the sun. This means that the sun is a central point around which
the _____ swing in a generally circular or _____
pattern. Think of a _____ swinging very slowly around
its _____. The _____ also _____ or
spin as they _____. This means that they turn around a line,
or _____, that runs through the center of the _____.
Think of how a _____ player _____ the ball on
the _____ of his _____, or how a top _____
on the floor. Our Earth _____ once every 24 hours, and it takes
365 and a half days to _____ the sun.

Figure 2.3: Reading passage with many unknown words.

You probably struggled to make meaning of this third-grade-level passage, which essentially illustrates how a reader who knows only the two thousand most common words in English would see it. The missing 15 percent of words have been removed because they are the least frequently used words that appear in this text, and such a reader won't know them.

Let's adjust this slightly. Try reading the passage as shown in figure 2.4.

Planets

All the planets revolve around, or orbit, the sun. This means that the sun
is a central point around which the planets swing in a generally circular
or _____. Think of a _____ swinging very slowly
around its pole. The planets also _____ or spin as they revolve.
This means that they turn around a line, or _____, that runs
through the center of the planet. Think of how a basketball player twirls the
ball on the tip of his finger, or how a top spins on the floor. Our
Earth _____ once every 24 hours, and it takes 365 and a half days
to orbit the sun.

Figure 2.4: Reading passage with a few unknown words.

You are likely feeling much more comfortable about your understanding of what you read. The text in figure 2.4 represents when a reader knows 98 percent of the words in a text. At this level of known words, two important things happen. First, even without knowledge of the unknown words, readers' general comprehension is fairly high. Second, with the context provided by both the known words and general comprehension, readers become far more capable of guessing the meaning of unknown words. At this point, both comprehension and optimum vocabulary acquisition occur. The question now is how to get students to learn enough words. In the following sections, we'll discuss the strengths and weaknesses of explicit vocabulary instruction and implicit vocabulary learning.

The Limitations of Direct Vocabulary Instruction

Vocabulary is embedded in the essence of reading in every genre. That makes implicit learning a no-brainer vocabulary development best practice. Yet many teachers maintain the practice of focusing on a weekly list of selected vocabulary words, which has, unfortunately, proven mostly ineffective. Words without context are just there: "The relation between thought and word is a living process; thought is born through words. A word devoid of thought is a dead thing, and a thought unembodied in words remains a shadow" (Vygotsky, 1986, p. 153). Put another way, when we provide words and dictionary definitions separate from full texts or conversations, context is lacking, and "words, in isolation, are ambiguous" (Willingham, 2017, p. 79). Teachers should try hard to vary their vocabulary teaching techniques and strategies and avoid traditional ones that mainly depend on memorization (Al-Darayseh, 2014).

A profound truth about vocabulary that we teachers must acknowledge is we cannot teach our students enough of it. Direct instruction may be appropriate for particular projects or units of study in order for students to use and see certain words, but it is literally impossible for a teacher to *directly* teach students the quantity of words they need to know to be highly successful. In the following provocative passage from *Invitation to a Beheading*, Vladimir Nabokov (1959) uses several words that students most likely do not learn as explicit vocabulary:

> So we are nearing the end. The right-hand, still untasted part of the novel, which, during our delectable reading, we would lightly feel, mechanically testing whether there was still plenty left (and our fingers were always gladdened by the placid, faithful thickness), has suddenly, for no reason at all, become quite meager: a few minutes of quick reading, already downhill, and—O horrible! (p. 12)

Students likely learn some of these words incidentally, seen and heard along the way in various places as implicit vocabulary. In particular, students might not know *delectable*, *gladdened*, or *meager*, yet many middle and secondary students could figure them out from the text if they realize the text is about reading a text. (That's a big *if*, isn't it?) According to Willingham (2017), "Much of the vocabulary we know is not the product of explicit study, but was learned incidentally, either through conversation or reading" (p. 98). In fact, more learning is implicit than we acknowledge (Willingham, 2017).

Isabel L. Beck, Margaret G. McKeown, and Linda Kucan (2013) estimate that students are capable of learning four hundred words each year through direct instruction, but Hirsch (2003) asserts that to get into a selective college, students should be learning five thousand words every year. Beck et al. (2013) suggest that knowledge of fifteen thousand *word families* (for example, *produce*, *production*, and *reproduce*) suffices, with eight thousand of those comprising "Tier One [words], the most familiar, everyday, spoken words that need little or no instruction" (p. 10).

While vocabulary experts offer differing suggestions for the ultimate size of the overall vocabulary necessary for overall success, they do agree that there is an appreciable gap between what students need and what we can directly teach. As researchers Gina N. Cervetti, Tanya S. Wright, and HyeJin Hwang (2016) succinctly state, "It is not possible to directly instruct enough words to close the word knowledge gap" (pp. 773–774), particularly for students with limited exposure to literacy at home. In short, we must have other means, beyond direct instruction, to aid vocabulary acquisition. Independent reading is a highly overlooked tool to consider.

We should note that Beck et al. (2013), leaders in the vocabulary field, are not as adamant about the role of independent reading in vocabulary acquisition as are we and multiple others cited here. They note that two conditions are necessary for students to learn vocabulary through reading. First, "students must read widely enough" and second, "students must have the skills to infer word meaning information from the contexts they read" (Beck et al., 2013, p. 5). Their concern is about struggling readers who "are less able to derive meaningful information from the context" (Beck et al., 2013, p. 5). They assert that "struggling readers do not read well enough to make wide reading an option" (Beck et al., 2013, p. 8). Instead, they greatly favor discussions of direct vocabulary instruction—their area of intense interest and study.

We do not accept their concerns about independent reading, nor do many others. We believe that the practices of developing background knowledge and stirring up prior knowledge are remarkable strategies that alleviate these concerns and honor the power of implicit vocabulary learning. Also, a hallmark of more structured approaches to independent reading is serious consideration of text complexity in order for teachers to make sure that students read accessible texts. We teachers should not pit vocabulary instruction against vocabulary acquisition through reading in an either–or conversation when the truth is that all readers, and struggling readers especially, need both. We need to avail ourselves of every tool, and independent reading is a powerful one.

Organically Effective: Implicit Learning of Vocabulary

Whether we encourage implicit acquisition of words through context clues or through memorization of a list of relevant vocabulary for a particular project, any chance to add words is beneficial. The implicit goal of the highly proficient reader is to attain a vast vocabulary. It follows that intellectual growth is contingent on mastering the social means of thought—that is, language (Vygotsky, 1986). Implicit learning of thousands of words is surely the lifeblood of literacy that translates directly into our lexicon through language.

Coming across a particularly precious word while reading is like discovering a treasure. Sometimes, known words jump out at readers as especially delicious ones that suit their palates. Other times, readers encounter uncommon and unknown words, those they might silently attempt to pronounce, take a second glance at for some sign of recognition, or just skip as they skim for context clues. Cervetti et al. (2016) note, "Learning words incidentally through reading and listening to text has the greatest potential to build" vocabulary (pp. 773–774). We, as teachers, should always encourage students to use the clues implied in their reading texts to develop their general language proficiency with words and improve their reading comprehension skills in particular (Al-Darayseh, 2014). To effectively help students build truly robust vocabularies, we must create the dynamics for students to self-teach.

A survey of the literature on acquiring vocabulary through reading is full of references to the work of Richard C. Anderson and William E. Nagy (1993). These prominent researchers have explored vocabulary acquisition through reading and reached significant findings. Anderson and Nagy (1993) assert that when students are reading at their independent reading levels, or the level at which they can read fluently, about 2 percent of the words they encounter will be unfamiliar if they are on the appropriate level. On their own, students will determine the meaning of about one in twenty of those unfamiliar words. While reading at an appropriate independent reading level, they will acquire roughly one new vocabulary word for every one thousand words that they read (Anderson & Nagy, 1993).

According to William E. Nagy and Patricia A. Herman (1984), "Once children can read, reading provides the major substrate for vocabulary growth" (as cited in Castles et al., 2018, p. 29). This rate of acquisition exceeds that at which we could directly teach vocabulary, but it is also predicated on students *reading*, and as we shared before, many students are not.

Figure 2.5 shows the cumulative number of words students read across the years of school. The darkest line represents students reading less than fifteen minutes a day. The medium line represents students reading between fifteen and twenty-nine minutes a day. And the lightest line represents students who read for more than thirty minutes a day.

Implicit Learning: Vocabulary Acquisition Through Reading

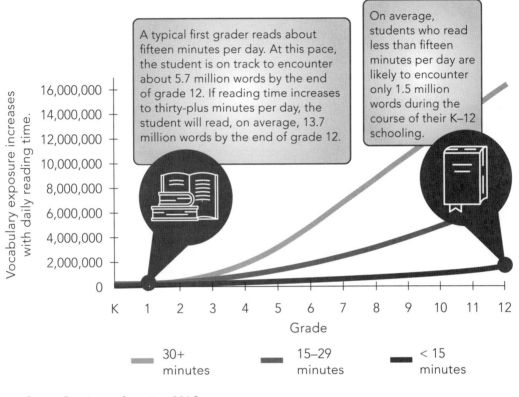

Source: Renaissance Learning, 2016.

Figure 2.5: Students' vocabulary acquisition based on cumulative words read.

As figure 2.5 states, students reading fewer than fifteen minutes daily will read roughly 1.5 million words across their years of school. Anderson and Nagy's (1993) research, then, would suggest that while doing so, they will acquire about 1,500 new vocabulary words. In contrast, those reading fifteen to twenty-nine minutes per day would cumulatively read 5.7 million words and thereby acquire 5,700 new vocabulary words. That's a gap of 4,200 words! Knowing the profound impact vocabulary has on reading comprehension, it's easy to understand how much further the students with the larger vocabularies will progress.

Reading also supplements any direct instruction on vocabulary that we might provide, as words appear in context in books. In their reading, students will encounter words on which they received direct instruction, and those words will be contextualized. This is critical because, as Willingham (2017) notes, words "derive their meaning from context" (p. 79). As we already noted, words apart from full texts or conversations lack context and can be ambiguous (Willingham, 2017).

Willingham (2017) illustrates this with an example that he terms a *lexical near-miss*. A dictionary might define *spill* as a verb meaning "to move or spread out into a wider place or area" ("Spill," n.d.). When asked to use the word in a sentence, a student might write, "This sandwich would be better if I had spilled the peanut butter to the edge of the bread" (Willingham, 2017, pp. 78–79). Clearly, the student has not fully understood the nuances of the word *spill*. And, as teachers, we have all observed something similar—students who know the dictionary definition of a word but still do not understand what it really means.

As tools for vocabulary acquisition, dictionaries have significant shortcomings. Beck et al. (2013) claim that "traditional definitions are not an effective vehicle for learning word meanings" (p. 43), and they provide an extensive dialogue in their work as to why. Beck et al. (2013) favor learner's dictionaries, which "were developed specifically for students learning English as a second language, but they are useful to any student of the language" (p. 48). Unlike traditional dictionaries, learner's dictionaries "present definitions in much more accessible language" and "provide discursive explanations for words rather than traditional definitions" while emphasizing absolute brevity (Beck et al., 2013, p. 48).

"Don't forget run-on. I use those all the time."

Source: © Mark Anderson, www.andertoons.com. Used with permission.

As Willingham (2017) notes, traditional "dictionaries can't specify all contexts, and so seek to offer context-free definitions. That's why they will inevitably be incomplete" (p. 79) as tools for vocabulary acquisition. While dictionaries can't provide context, reading can and does, making it not only an efficient means of acquiring vocabulary but an invaluable one. So, through wide independent reading, students—and actually all readers, throughout their lives—can continue to add new words to their vocabulary—their personal dictionaries.

Classroom Applications for Teachers

How can we embrace vocabulary and the look of reading in the classroom? We include here brief knowledge-centric classroom lessons that are applicable for preK–3, grades 4–6, grades 7–8, and grades 9–12 and that highlight the look of literacy. Teachers can try these sample lessons in their own classrooms and tailor them to the key knowledge pieces their students are studying. In other words, teachers can connect the lessons to their own curriculum.

Mrs. Wyman's First-Grade Class

The focus of reading instruction in this preK–3 class is on *one word at a time*—mostly nouns and verbs, as they are the first concrete units of literacy for young students entering the world of words and stories. To achieve this, Mrs. Wyman uses an activity called Shoebox Curriculum, which is based on British teacher Sylvia Ashton-Warner's (1963) *key vocabulary model* of using the native language of Maori students in New Zealand. Ashton-Warner realized that her students had no connection to British English, so she devised her own watercolor primers, allowing students to use familiar native words. Ashton-Warner's (1963) method involves a knowledge-centric curriculum that she developed with her K–8 Maori students, using guided reading, oral reading, student-to-student reading, and extensive daily student writing. Her innovative approach to working with nonreaders of all grade levels was adopted by U.S. teachers. Mrs. Wyman starts her first graders off with a full literacy program of phonics awareness and practice and personal vocabulary building.

Mrs. Wyman's Shoebox Curriculum is designed to show just how independent students can be when structures are in place to encourage self-direction and flexibility. To prepare for this activity, Mrs. Wyman provides time for students to decorate their shoeboxes in creative ways. The main ingredient of every shoebox is a sentence book, which is a folded paper booklet of blank pages that will soon hold students' drawings and writing. The boxes will also hold word cards that students collect; they get a new one every day. The students store their shoeboxes on a designated shelf in the classroom and retrieve them every morning upon arrival.

The Shoebox Curriculum is a monthly cycle that consists of the following daily steps.

1. The day begins with exercises that stir students' prior knowledge. That prior knowledge may yield a special word they want to study and add to the collection of past words in their word box.

2. Students play a variation of the card game Go Fish with a partner. Both players dump out their word cards, then take turns drawing them. The player who draws the card reads the word out loud and then says whether the word is his or hers.

3. Students receive their daily word during a miniconference with the teacher. During this time, Mrs. Wyman reminds them to be on the lookout for new words they want to use.

4. Students study their words in one of several centers set up around the classroom—a painting easel, a corner with blocks, a tub of sand, the chalkboard, and so on.

5. Back at their desks, students take their sentence books from their shoeboxes and begin their daily work, which includes drawing pictures of the word and writing sentences using the word.

6. Students pair up with their partners once again and read their sentences aloud to each other.

At the end of the month, Mrs. Wyman signals that it's time for students to take their sentence booklets home to share. Their assignment is to read them aloud; the audience might be family members, friends, neighbors, pets, stuffed animals, or even themselves in the mirror. The process includes plenty of reading, writing, speaking, and listening, and allows students to apply what they are learning about in phonics in order to build their personal vocabulary.

Teachers who use this approach may find themselves inspired as well. Figure 2.6 features a poem inspired by the experience of implementing Ashton-Warner's (1963) organic model, telling the story of how students learned to read and write with rigorous yet exhilarating daily routines.

The Shoebox Curriculum is an opportunity for students to *implicitly* learn words by word choice and *explicitly* learn them with direct word study. The complete process replicates a knowledge-centric curriculum as we have stressed throughout the entire book. Student work that results from this activity truly illustrates the richness of their vocabulary and the remarkable stories they tell. Visit www.robinfogarty.com /literacyreframed for a wealth of student examples.

Deep Inside of Me: For Wee Ones

I start with just one word,
One special word,
Way down deep inside of me
A word I love,
A word I fear,
One I can see,
And touch, and hear.
I start with just one word,
One special word,
Way down deep inside of me.

Now I tell just what
That one can do . . .
Popcorn pops,
Jackrabbit hops
Grass grows,
Birdy flew,
Bluebird sings,
But bee stings.
Now I tell . . . just what
That one can do . . .

Hmmm, now
That I have two,
Why not
Add + a + few?
I tell its color . . .
And shape
And size.
I create a picture of words
For your eyes.

Hmmm, now that I have two,
Why not add + a + few?

By gosh, by golly, by gee,
I've got a whole story
Way down deep
Inside of me . . .
A story of love
Or one of fear,
One I can touch and say and hear.
By gosh, by golly, by gee
Indeed! Indeed! Indeed!
I've got all the words I need.
There's a whole story
Way down deep inside of me
Indeed! Indeed! Indeed!
I have all the words I need.

Believe it or not,
All those words that I've got
Can be set free
From way down deep inside of me.
They can be thought about
Or better yet, said right out,
And if I write them down
I'll have a story to say and see
A real story to really read
From way down deep inside of me.
Believe it or not,
All those words that I've got
Can be set free
From way down deep inside of me.

Source: © 1989 by Robin Fogarty.

Figure 2.6: Poem for a literacy block of extensive reading and writing.

A teacher who uses the Shoebox Curriculum as described will have holistic, authentic artifacts of student growth and powerful "memoirs" that parents will treasure. This whole experience produces longitudinal portfolios of student growth. This strategy emphasizes learning to read and write by reading and writing. Many teachers intuitively teach reading using this method. As we have read, research supports this model focused on prior knowledge and background experience as a high-growth approach. A variation of this strategy could be to scan the students' artwork or have the students record themselves reading their writing and then upload the products to the class website.

Mr. Juarez's Sixth-Grade Class

Intermediate learners transition in their literacy work from a focus on phonics, oral reading, and spelling and writing practices into more extensive content-area reading with more sophisticated texts, fewer pictures, and more tables and graphics, as well as essay writing and projects and performances with more speaking and listening. They are beyond everyday words, and their vocabularies have expanded widely, just as their world has.

These classroom sessions focus on literacy and playfulness with the look and sound of words and language. They invoke student experiments in sounding out unusual words as well as attempts to make meaning of the words as students try to comprehend a nonsense poem. Mr. Juarez's goal is for his students to appreciate and delight in words; by this time in their reading lives, they have likely assessed themselves as either good or poor readers, and he wants to get them to enjoy reading with approaches that have rigor and relevance.

Session 1: Nonsense Words

Students at this age are familiar with words and are beginning to care about word choice. This Nonsense Words exercise introduces them to the creativity and exploration that are possible with language. The goal is to engage students in a frivolous task with an authentic outcome.

Mr. Juarez divides his sixth graders into pairs. Each pair reads from a large screen that displays the following poem, "Jabberwocky" by Lewis Carroll (1871). Mr. Juarez color-codes the poem's lines to show which partner reads which line and also to facilitate post-reading discussion:

> 'Twas brillig, and the slithy toves
> Did gyre and gimble in the wabe:
> All mimsy were the borogoves,
> And the mome raths outgrabe.
>
> "Beware the Jabberwock, my son!
> The jaws that bite, the claws that catch!
> Beware the Jubjub bird, and shun
> The frumious Bandersnatch!"
>
> He took his vorpal sword in hand;
> Long time the manxome foe he sought—
> So rested he by the Tumtum tree
> And stood awhile in thought.

And, as in uffish thought he stood,
The Jabberwock, with eyes of flame,
Came whiffling through the tulgey wood,
And burbled as it came!

One, two! One, two! And through and through
The vorpal blade went snicker-snack!
He left it dead, and with its head
He went galumphing back.

"And hast thou slain the Jabberwock?
Come to my arms, my beamish boy!
O frabjous day! Callooh! Callay!"
He chortled in his joy.

'Twas brillig, and the slithy toves
Did gyre and gimble in the wabe:
All mimsy were the borogoves,
And the mome raths outgrabe.

It is amazing to see students' enjoyment during the reading. The ultimate goal is for students to learn about word choice and sequencing, as well as develop the innate ability to somewhat decipher what a text is saying.

Session 2: Real Words for Nonsense Words

After the read-aloud of "Jabberwocky," student pairs rewrite the poem, replacing the nonsense words with real words they choose. The challenge is to use words that make sense and are consistent throughout the poem. A teacher might scaffold this lesson by providing some replacement words, but we caution against doing too much for the students so that they receive the opportunity to be creative.

In both versions of the Nonsense Words strategy, teachers can customize their applications by using a different poem with nonsense words or replacing the words of a different poem with nonsense words. The two versions could be consolidated into one session if that works better. In addition, at the end of the lesson, they could list the nonsense words on the board, and the students could come up and add the words they used to replace those nonsense words. This would create an artifact that very richly displays the students' vocabulary.

If teachers wanted to creatively transfer this strategy, they could have the student pairs read the nonsense poem and then, instead of changing the poem, write their own nonsense poems and exchange their poems with another pair of students to read and rewrite with new words. Another variation could involve putting the nonsense poem on the class website. Over a couple of days, students could each contribute their own version of the poem with new words. This would lead to a community of readers and writers expanding their vocabulary and engaging through collaboration.

Session 3: Break the Block

This Break the Block lesson requires students to consider the look or structure of what they are reading. First, in pairs, they research and write in one solid block an essay or a story about a topic that they are studying. They write in a stream of consciousness with punctuation but with no paragraphing; preferably, they do this on a computer so they could make later edits easier if they have time to do that. After the students have completed writing the block of text, and checked it, they will print their writing and exchange it with another pair of students. Student partners will then read each other's text block and edit with proper paragraphing. The student pairs may use the skill of close reading on their peers' paper, make changes to the paper, and then justify their chosen paragraph breaks.

Having students break a block is significantly different from simply having them edit each other's work, as this strategy does not cause students the anxiety that they might feel about their peers' reading their writing because the task is quite open-ended with many possible answers. The Break the Block strategy frees up the student writers so that they can more easily write something that their peers will have to edit. Writing a hard block of text becomes a challenge that students will be eager to take on because their peers will have to break the block.

This strategy may not seem worthwhile at first glance because, during lessons, teachers frequently discuss the need to break text into paragraphs for clarity. Here, students intentionally ignore those lessons when creating their block of text. It's just a new take on understanding paragraphing. The strategy builds in creativity by asking students to be the architects of this solid block of writing and do the exact opposite of what teachers normally ask them to do. Often, they find this minor switch quite exciting. Then, students read another pair's block and insert paragraph breaks as needed. This step helps students discern changes of subject, pace, tenor, or mood to clarify understanding for the reader.

Teachers can customize this activity to any subject area. They can have students break the block in social studies or science instead of just ELA. In addition, a more creative and, admittedly, more challenging way to transfer this strategy would be to have the students write with no punctuation instead of no paragraphing. A less extreme example could have students pick a block of text from a website and then remove the punctuation and formatting. Again, it piques student interest to be aware of the amount and type of punctuation in their reading and writing. The difference here is that the students know there are correct answers for them to determine because the original writing did have punctuation. Despite these wrinkles, students could, believe it or not, find it invigorating to analyze and properly punctuate the block of text, as students come to enjoy playing with words, structures, and literacy elements.

Mrs. Whitehall's Seventh-Grade English Class

Middle schoolers, well into reading textbooks, also use handheld technology to engage in all types of communication, so it follows that for them, the look of literacy is high in imagery, animation, font options, and color coding. Mrs. Whitehall uses two activities to engage students in the look of reading: (1) Vocabulary by Osmosis and (2) Words Matter, Just Ask Huck. This multisensory content includes the literature they read and also the literature and ideas they write or create. The result is an everyday vocabulary that has grown organically and, in some ways, unconsciously.

Session 1: Vocabulary by Osmosis

Students build a vast vocabulary through two very different means: (1) explicit instruction in academic vocabulary and (2) implicit acquisition of words. This exercise, Vocabulary by Osmosis, has students engage in a dialogue about these two ways to learn new vocabulary, and it guides students in understanding and appreciating extensive reading as a conduit for vocabulary acquisition.

Mrs. Whitehall divides the students into pairs, partner A and partner B, to provide the following partner-specific prompts to each other.

1. **Partner A:** How often do you read? Compare it with how often you read when you were younger. Also, how has your reading changed over the years?

2. **Partner B:** (Compare your answer to that same question with your partner's.)

3. **Partner B:** Who do you know who has a huge vocabulary? Describe how you know and how you think that person acquired a greater-than-normal vocabulary.

4. **Partner A:** (Compare your answer to that same question with your partner's.)

5. **Partners A and B:** Have a discussion about any new words that either of you has learned this week and how you learned them. Say if it was intentional or incidental learning. Talk about those ideas for a minute.

Vocabulary by Osmosis requires both partners to be good listeners in addition to using higher-order thinking to respond to the prompts. This A–B partner strategy is most effective when the second partner does not know what the assignment is until his or her partner has finished sharing the assigned prompt. This way, students have to be attentive, as they have no idea what they will have to say when it is their turn.

To customize this strategy, teachers just need to make the prompts' content correspond to their subject matter's vocabulary, or they could write different prompts. It works for just about any subject. For example, a history teacher could include the following prompts.

1. **Partner A:** Give three reasons that Thomas Jefferson authorized the Louisiana Purchase.

2. **Partner B:** Explain whether you agree or disagree with the reasons given.

Teachers can give this lesson three to four times throughout the year with similar questions. It encourages students to take a stand and offer a supported opinion.

Session 2: Words Matter, Just Ask Huck

For this strategy, Mrs. Whitehall selects a single passage from Mark Twain's (1884/2013) *The Adventures of Huckleberry Finn* that is rich in vocabulary and sometimes confusing in meaning:

> Mornings, before daylight, I slipped into cornfields and borrowed a watermelon, or a mushmelon, or a punkin, or some new corn, or things of that kind. Pap always said it warn't no harm to borrow things, if you was meaning to pay them back, some time; but the widow said it warn't anything but a soft name for stealing, and no decent body would do it. (p. 68)

She displays the passage on a projector screen for students to read three times. The first reading is a buddy reading, with A–B partners both reading aloud at once. In the second reading, A–B partners take turns reading aloud every other line. Finally, for the third reading, students read the paragraph to themselves.

After reading, students copy all the passage's nouns and verbs onto their own paper—partner A does nouns, and partner B does verbs. Then they talk about the words they have listed, focusing on special word choices as a challenge and making a comment about each one. Finally, students individually complete the Words Matter assignment by writing a paragraph describing whether they found this particular passage easy or hard to comprehend and their reasons why.

Finally, after sampling some of the responses, Mrs. Whitehall talks directly to students about the power of words, how words add spice to the reading, and how words can add a kick to the students' own writing. She encourages them to think about word choice and unusual vocabulary words that seem just right for what they're trying to say.

Mrs. Grayson's Tenth-Grade Speech and Debate Class

The academic skills of secondary students are developing and maturing as they read high-level texts in the various disciplines and write more scholarly essays supported by evidence. At the same time, digital reading and writing are fast taking over the helm of the look of literacy. For that reason, Mrs. Grayson uses two related sessions, one that uses pencil and paper, and the other that focuses on digital reading. We will explore digital reading in greater depth in chapter 4 (page 131).

Session 1: Paper to Podcast—Facts to Act On

Mrs. Grayson asks her students to each write a serious and comprehensive paper that illustrates the facts of a school issue that concerned leaders in their community and school district need to act on now. She provides an outline for developing the paper (research, organize, write, draft, read, revise, and summarize) and a list of ten issues from which students can select one to develop. The students study all these issues in class.

1. Dropouts
2. Opioids
3. Autism
4. Electronic cigarettes
5. Teen suicide
6. Dyslexia
7. Academic cheating
8. School violence
9. Reading success

Session 2: Podcast—Facts to Act On

Based on their writing assignment, students develop a five- to ten-minute podcast episode. Student pairs write a script, practice the timing of it by reading it out loud to each other, and actually record it. Mrs. Grayson's podcast series, *Facts to Act On*, helps spread the word about important school concerns and allows students to inform others and motivate themselves. This classroom or schoolwide project on issues under study is about using facts and the power of words to inspire action.

Teachers can easily copy this assignment using other selections not formerly used. As another customization, teachers could have students create a thirty-second public service announcement rather than a podcast. This way, students will have to be more precise with their language and more technically concise with the length of their audio product.

Teachers can also customize the lesson by changing the subject from current issues of concern to similar issues that occurred when their parents were in school. This makes it a compare-and-contrast exercise. Also, they can make this assignment more creative by asking students to imagine themselves in the year 2050 and think about what a major concern might be for future students.

PLC Discussion Questions

We provide these discussion questions for use within department or grade-level teams. If your school functions as a professional learning community, these questions are an effective way to encourage professional dialogue in your collaborative team. Conversations like this are key to building trust within the team and helping team members learn from one another. Choose one or several based on interest and concerns exposed during a book study or independent reading of this book.

- How does the research on self-teaching change how your collaborative team answers the question, "What do we want all students to know and be able to do?" (DuFour et al., 2016).

- Discuss how teachers can teach students to define orthographic representations as part of reading instruction, and how teachers can increase the amount of time that students practice this skill.

- In what way could you share with students how you, as an adult, have recently engaged in self-teaching by sounding out words to yourself?

- What are some ways that classroom teachers can create the necessary conditions for self-teaching?

- Reconsider this quote from Willingham (2017): "Reluctant readers read 50,000 words each year, . . . avid readers encounter many more words— as many as 4,000,000" (p. 68). Where do the readers in your classroom or school fall on the scale between reluctant readers and avid readers?

- Reconsider the following statement: "We teachers should not pit vocabulary instruction against vocabulary acquisition through reading in an either–or conversation when the truth is that all readers, and struggling readers especially, need both. We need to avail ourselves of every tool, and independent reading is a powerful one." Do you agree or disagree with this statement? Give two reasons why.

- How will what you have learned in this chapter change your approach to teaching vocabulary?

Resources for Learning More

In an excellent thirty-minute presentation (available at https://bit.ly/3k5VZrY), cognitive neuroscientist Stanislas Dehaene explains how the brain learns to read (WISE Channel, 2013).

The Reading Mind: A Cognitive Approach to Understanding How the Mind Reads by Daniel T. Willingham (2017) is a fabulous read. As we've mentioned, Willingham's work on reading and understanding how the brain learns to read has been a major source for our work on this book. He is knowledgeable, current, and easy to read, and his ideas are ripe for implementation.

CHAPTER 3

The Knowingness of Reading— Background Knowledge

We write [and read] to taste life twice, in the
moment and in retrospection.

—Anaïs Nin

Mr. Brown shares the classic children's story *Wilfrid Gordon McDonald Partridge* (Fox, 1984) with his class. In this story, a precocious young boy named Wilfrid is upset when he hears that Miss Nancy Alison Delacourt Cooper is losing her memory. He goes into action. He gathers a bunch of things—a warm egg, a medal, some shells—in a big flower basket. When he visits Miss Nancy, he pulls the items out one by one and shows them to Miss Nancy to help her get her memory back. After Mr. Brown reads this story about the power of memory to his students, the class visits www.storylineonline.net/books/wilfrid -gordon-mcdonald-partridge (Storyline Online, 2012) to see and hear actor Bradley Whitford read the story out loud. Just thinking about this wonderful tale, so beautifully rendered in Mem Fox's (1984) book, provokes the reader to consider what knowledge is all about and how it transforms, at some point, into maturity. Knowledge comes, but knowingness lingers.

After chapters 1 and 2's refreshing discussions about literacy's practical functions (decoding and vocabulary) and aesthetic inspirations (melodic sounds and vivid visuals that illustrate the charming, compelling, and at times challenging fundamentals of reading), we now turn (or swipe) the page to the final and most enduring element of literacy: knowingness, the permanent knowledge we take away from reading. According to Hirsch (2003), "Fluent decoding is an absolute prerequisite," but research on the role of knowledge in effective reading shows us that "comprehension—the goal of decoding—won't improve unless we also pay serious attention to building our students' word and world knowledge" (p. 20). Therefore, it's important to know that fluency is a key to comprehension: the evidence, in fact, that we know or have learned something. These elements—decoding, fluency, and comprehension—are almost symbiotic in reading excellence.

Throughout our exploration of the sound of literacy, we addressed decoding—the absolute prerequisite of literacy. In our discussion of the look of literacy, we explored the acquisition of word knowledge. Now, we will come to understand that the knowingness of literacy is what is stored in our memories in our own unique way that makes sense to us at the time of storage and at the time of retrieval. It may not be difficult to store a quantity of facts in one's short-term memory, but the ability to form judgments about those facts requires hard work and the tempering heat of experience and maturity. This is the difference between knowledge we acquire and the knowingness of our interpretation that we store away. That knowingness stored in long-term memory connects through neural activity that makes sense at the time, and thus becomes background knowledge within a known pattern of existing knowledge. That said, the systematic development of knowledge warrants consideration within our daily work as educators. Knowledge builds knowledge, and it actually makes learning and knowingness cumulative as we consolidate and exponentially grow it.

Surveying Knowingness

This playful but mindful survey of why, what, when, where, how, and whom we read is a reflective and metacognitive conversation about how we learn. This kind of introspective thinking sharpens our insights about ourselves.

Why We Read

We can read to inform, to educate, to entertain, to communicate; we read because it was recommended or we liked the title, the cover, the inspired thinking and inferences, the comparisons, predictions, and the obvious and not so obvious implications.

Essayist Anaïs Nin (1974) writes, "We write to taste life twice, in the moment, and in retrospection. We write, like Proust, to render all of it eternal, and to persuade ourselves that it is eternal" (pp. 149–150). We strongly believe that the same is true of reading, hence the modification we made to Nin's quote in this chapter's epigraph.

What We Read

We read fiction that includes literature, poetry, scripts, lyrics, novels, short stories, novellas, and much more. And we read nonfiction that includes newspapers, blogs, emails, tweets, letters, textbooks, articles, editorials, documents, primary sources, vintage books, manuscripts, and much more.

In the broadest, most encompassing sense, we can read words, stars, faces, golf greens, tea leaves, lyrics, body language, schedules, calendars, gravestones, character traits, gestures, genres, eras, types, styles, interests, passions, sign language, and mathematical symbols, to name a few. In essence, these things we can read in passing as we interact with the world.

When We Read

We can read in the morning, at noon, and at night; in the spring, summer, fall, and winter; and when we're bored, curious, studying, traveling, vacationing, relaxing, searching, stopping to think, and glancing. We can read all the time, any time, and . . . never.

Where We Read

We can read on a train, on a plane, in a car, at home, at school, at a restaurant, in church, on a park bench, in a library, in the theater, in the waiting room, in the attic, by the sea, in the ski lodge, on a sailboat, and in the hammock. Reading is an all-weather, all-location, all-consuming pastime and when deeply engaged in it, it stirs our minds and touches our souls.

How We Read

How do we read? Let us list the ways. We can read online and on paper, in spurts and all at once. We can read by skimming or by reading closely, critically, and analytically. We can read within disciplines; reading about science could include biology, physics, chemistry, earth science, or astronomy. And we can read alone, with book clubs, in classroom pairs, with partners, or with music in the background. We can read any way we want in the moment.

Whom We Read

We can read a variety of authors from diverse backgrounds. We find our favorites often through the genres and subjects we prefer. Agatha Christie (mysteries), Stephen King (suspense and horror), Maya Angelou (poetry), Nnedi Okorafor (science fiction), Mem Fox (children's literature), Richard Wright (social justice, prejudice, and race), Henry Wadsworth Longfellow (1909; highlighting of diverse voices with works such as "The Song of Hiawatha"), and the list goes on and on and on. Once we are really readers, we know our list of favorites and may even add others as we continue our reading.

Knowledge: A Million Miles Wide, Inches Deep

Knowingness has its own story. It's the story of knowing ignited by our experiences, our reading, our conversations, our loves and fears, our explorations, and our distillations of fact. Knowingness is our way of expressing what we have retained, learned, practiced, and shared using our own words, connections, and patterns of thought. It's knowledge transformed into knowingness that governs our words, actions, and deeds. It belongs directly to the person who developed it. In other words, knowingness is one's own take on the more universal view of knowledge learned. Knowingness can interchangeably refer to *knowledge-based content*, *discipline-specific content*, and simply *content-based reading*. Used as an all-encompassing word, *knowingness* focuses on the results and awareness of reading and learning, instead of delineating the process of reading.

In his book *Why Knowledge Matters*, Hirsch (2018) defines *general knowledge* as the universal common knowledge that everyone should know to become what we traditionally consider culturally literate. This knowledge is far different from either the knowledge we might label as trivia or the exceedingly deep, content-specific knowledge of the expert (Hirsch, 2018). In sum, cultural literacy is the body of knowledge that is commonly known within a specific, well-defined cultural group.

Baseball and Background Knowledge

In the introduction (page 1), we saw how one can know all the words in a text and still not understand the text's meaning. This phenomenon illustrates the role of knowledge in reading comprehension. Pimentel (2018) refers to research in this area as "some of the most profoundly important, yet under-recognized, reading research" available and asserts that "the implications for literacy instruction are enormous." Let's build up our understanding of the role of knowledge here and then explore those enormous implications.

A variety of experiments have explored the role of knowledge in reading comprehension and discovered something almost counterintuitive. *Low-performing* readers have outscored *high-performing* readers on reading comprehension tasks. How can this be? At first, these results seem to defy logic. But the constructs of these studies offer tremendous insights because they show that knowledge is more powerfully related to reading comprehension than either general reading ability or IQ.

In one experiment, researchers Donna R. Recht and Lauren Leslie (1988) broke a group of sixty-four middle school students from grades 7 and 8 in the same metropolitan school into four subgroups based on two factors: (1) reading ability (low and high) and (2) knowledge of baseball (low and high). This resulted in four groups.

1. High-performing readers who know a lot about baseball

2. High-performing readers who know little about baseball

3. Low-performing readers who know a lot about baseball

4. Low-performing readers who know little about baseball

All students read a domain-specific passage on baseball and then completed a variety of activities to document comprehension. In short, the researchers pitted knowledge against reading ability to determine which was more predictive of performance. The results were quite informative (see figure 3.1).

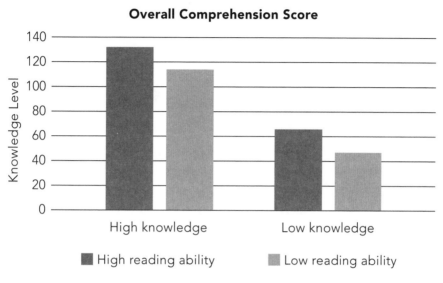

Overall Comprehension Score

Source: Recht & Leslie, 1988.

Figure 3.1: Comparison of reading comprehension performance by reading ability and by background knowledge.

Recht and Leslie (1988) find that, when it comes to reading domain-specific texts, *background knowledge* of the subject is a significantly stronger predictor of performance than *reading ability* is. Low-performing readers who had background knowledge about baseball easily outperformed high-performing readers who knew little about the subject. And, for the two groups with little background knowledge, those with high reading ability did only marginally better than those with low reading ability. *Background knowledge of a text's subject is a stronger predictor of performance than reading ability.*

Researchers Wolfgang Schneider, Joachim Körkel, and Franz E. Weinert (1989) took a very similar approach with a group of elementary students reading a passage on soccer. However, they divided students based on high and low IQ as opposed to high and low reading ability. Their results were very similar to those of Recht and Leslie (1988; see figure 3.2, page 92). Low-IQ students who had knowledge of the topic notably outperformed high-IQ students who did not. Between the two low-knowledge groups, the high-IQ students were able to correctly answer only one more question (out of sixteen total questions) than their low-IQ counterparts could.

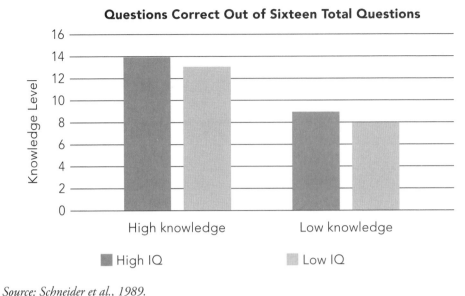

Questions Correct Out of Sixteen Total Questions

Source: Schneider et al., 1989.

Figure 3.2: Comparison of reading comprehension performance by IQ and by background knowledge.

These two studies, still widely cited in recent research, began the current exploration of the role of knowledge in reading comprehension that continues. Researchers Diana J. Arya, Elfrieda H. Hiebert, and P. David Pearson (2011) exposed a group of third-grade students to a variety of texts that included topics *familiar* to them (for example, jellybeans and toothpaste) and others *unfamiliar* to them (for example, tree frogs and soil) and then tracked comprehension in relation to text complexity. Their results showed that "when the topics were familiar . . . the complexity of the text had little effect on accuracy or speed of comprehension" (Arya et al., 2011, as cited in Hirsch, 2018, p. 89). They found that "text complexity is shrugged off and unfamiliar words are rightly guessed when the topic is familiar" (Arya et al., 2011, as cited in Hirsch, 2018, p. 89). These insights make the case for building background knowledge as a prominent strategy to improve reading facility.

Finally, Wexler (2019) summarizes the work of Tanya Kaefer, Susan B. Neuman, and Ashley M. Pinkham (2015) in the following:

> Researchers read preschoolers from mixed socioeconomic backgrounds a book about birds, a subject they had determined the higher-income kids already knew more about. When they tested comprehension, the wealthier children did significantly better. But then they read a story about a subject neither group knew anything about: made-up animals called *wugs*. When prior knowledge was equalized, comprehension [between the two groups] was essentially the same. In other words, the

gap in comprehension wasn't a gap in skills. *It was a gap in knowledge.* (as cited in Wexler, 2019, p. 30, emphasis added)

These are not the only studies. As Willingham (2017) notes, "In other experiments reading skill *does* make a contribution, but it's often relatively small, and it's *virtually always smaller* than the importance of topic knowledge" (p. 122). Hirsch (2018) boldly states, "Once decoding has been mastered and fluency attained, relevant knowledge becomes the chief component of reading skill. Every cognitive scientist specializing in the subject would agree with that statement" (p. 23).

> *"When prior knowledge was equalized, comprehension [between the two groups] was essentially the same. In other words, the gap in comprehension wasn't a gap in skills. It was a gap in knowledge" (Kaefer et al., 2015, as cited in Wexler, 2019, p. 30).*

Similarly, Hirsch (2018) asserts, "Knowledge is by far the most promising avenue to carry us out of the reading slump we are in" and "is by far the most promising way to advance reading skill for all" (p. 31). He adds that schools should come to the following realization:

> The secret to answering [the complex questions of today's high-stakes tests] will not be hours of practice of "inferencing skills" and "close reading skills," but can only be answered through the student's prior relevant knowledge of the words and the topics. (Hirsch, 2018, p. 30)

Yet, in a misguided attempt to raise reading scores, we cut time from the social studies and science classes that provide precious knowledge, and we are so busy teaching reading strategies and covering all the standards that we devote little time to some of the best activities to build vocabulary. "No matter how well-trained students become in main-idea finding, the student with the smaller relevant vocabulary and knowledge is the one who will fare worse on the test" (Hirsch, 2018, p. 23).

These insights allow us to look at text complexity in a deeper way. Many educators rely on readability formulas alone to convey the difficulty of a text, but it seems that knowledge is as powerful a determinant of text difficulty as readability is. Hirsch (2018) contends that readability formulas convey *theoretical difficulty*, while *actual difficulty* depends on what knowledge the reader brings to the text. Based on what knowledge a student already possesses, he or she can be "an excellent reader about dinosaurs and a terrible reader about mushrooms" (Hirsch, 2018, p. 75).

It seems somewhat conclusive that while much of educators' attention has been on reading strategies, skills, and standards, as a professional group, we must come to understand that "no amount of strategy instruction can bring about successful comprehension if the text cannot be understood because of limitations in knowledge" (Castles et al., 2018, p. 36). As Wexler (2019) notes, "Comprehension, unlike decoding, doesn't occur as a result of teaching students a set of skills they then practice repeatedly. It's something people achieve more or less naturally—*if they have enough information*" (p. 47, emphasis added). It's akin to osmosis, to return to an earlier lesson example. Learners who are motivated to be readers seem to soak up knowledge through an environment that stimulates curiosity and the desire to know. Yet how much focus do we give to the acquisition of knowledge? We must adopt a different posture about promoting the behavior of wanting to know and adapting the school curriculum to honor and support that kind of student-centered, knowledge-rich approach to learning.

To give students the background knowledge they need, teachers must create learning conditions that foster curiosity and afford time for the search for knowledge about whatever commands students' interests. This shift only can follow if teachers, administrators, and formal institutions demonstrate, through their priorities, that wanting to know, learning, and gaining knowledge deserve as much time as possible in the academic day. It means discussing, sorting, prioritizing, and installing social-emotional learning, such as the growth mindset, neuroscience about how we learn, and multiple catalysts that truly foster student agency.

Massive Amounts of General Information

The comprehension of readers who have poor background knowledge will always suffer, regardless of their general reading abilities. This is because, as Willingham (2017) notes, "Writers always omit a great deal of information needed to make sense of what they write" (p. 116). He offers the following as an illustration:

> "The morning precipitation had left sidewalks icy. Kayla told her children to be careful." The connection seems simple to see; the icy sidewalks caused Kayla to say that to her children. But consider all of the knowledge the reader had to bring to those sentences to make that causal connection:
> The morning precipitation had left sidewalks icy.
> People walk on sidewalks.
> Ice is slippery.
> People can fall when walking on slippery surfaces.
> People can be hurt if they fall.
> Parents don't want their children to be hurt.
> People are less likely to fall if they walk carefully.
> Kayla told her children to be careful. (Willingham, 2017, p. 116)

If writers could not assume readers have a general knowledge base that is "a million miles wide, but just a few inches deep" (Willingham, 2017, p. 118), then their writing would have to be unwieldy and boring. Writers "judge what their readers already know and what must be made explicit in the text, and they write accordingly" (Willingham, 2017, p. 116).

In the real world, the information required for comprehension is more dynamic than in this simple example, but the concept is the same: "The meaning of a text is constructed from both presented information and reader-contributed information" (Hirsch, 2018, p. 88). Writers make assumptions about what readers likely know. If readers have the assumed information, comprehension occurs. If not, all meaning could be lost. Consider the following simple sentences and the knowledge they assume.

- "It was a herculean task."
- "They reacted like Pavlov's dogs."
- "That became her Waterloo moment."
- "You're tilting at windmills."

To fully comprehend what the writer of these sentences is conveying, readers need specific knowledge about a wide range of topics, from classical mythology to literature to history. As a result, we teachers must articulate what composes the miles-wide and inches-deep general knowledge with opportunities to stir up prior knowledge and uncover the most urgent information for that reading. However, we must also structure thinking by using pair shares or similar experiences for students to learn from other students (Willingham, 2017). What names, dates, places, people, and ideas do students need to know to be literate in the world?

The Matthew Effect

Addressing the need for knowledge will significantly help teachers address persistent achievement gaps. Many discussions about such gaps reference the *Matthew effect*. This concept is based on the following Bible verse: "For whosoever hath, to him shall be given, and he shall have more abundance: but whosoever hath not, from him shall be taken away even that he hath" (Matthew 13:12, King James Version). Loosely paraphrased, this verse is familiar to many as the aphorism, "The rich get richer and the poor get poorer." When we understand the role of knowledge in comprehension, the Matthew effect applies perfectly: readers with a lot of knowledge become even better readers, and readers who lack knowledge fall further and further behind.

"Clearly you're smart. But are you *book* smart?"

Source: © Mark Anderson, www.andertoons.com. Used with permission.

Some students come to school rich in knowledge. Before they could read, they were read to. Once they could read, they were encouraged and supported in doing so. They have visited museums and historical sites, and they have traveled to other cities, other states, or even other countries. Because of the knowledge they have, they take away more from every school lesson, lecture, video, field trip, or other educational experience than their classmates do. As Hirsch (2018) remarks, "The early knowledge base that has been gained by fortunate students is like Velcro; it is a base to which further knowledge sticks more readily" (p. 164). They are rich, and they get richer.

In contrast, other students come to school poor in knowledge. They were seldom, if ever, read to and might not even have a single book. Their home conditions or the responsibilities they bear (such as helping care for younger siblings) are not conducive to wide independent reading, and if they do have the time and inclination to read, they may have few books on hand. They have rarely left their immediate neighborhoods or towns, so their world concept is limited. As a result, they take away far less from the same educational experiences that their rich-in-knowledge classmates thrive on. They can be sitting in the same classroom, and while the knowledge-rich classmates beside them get richer, they fall further behind.

Referencing the Matthew effect, Hirsch (2018) notes, "For most students, the period of the primary school is the latest time when the Apostle can be proved wrong, when the have-nots in knowledge and vocabulary can still be transformed into haves" (p. 164). He contends that teachers have no time to waste. We must address knowledge deficits as quickly as possible because "content delay in the early years is harmful to all and disastrous to the disadvantaged" (Hirsch, 2018, p. 165). Students must arrive at a school that is well prepared to deliver a thoughtful, knowledge-rich curriculum, but curriculum documents vary in specificity, and even the word *curriculum* holds multiple meanings. We will address the critical need for clear curricula shortly.

The Desire for More Knowledge

Curiosity, again. We humans are curious beings, with a primitive part of our brain that instinctively notices differences on the horizon. When it's not stressed, that part of our brain triggers natural responses that urge us to want to know more (Willis, 2016). Our quest for knowingness is real. And that is the prevailing motivation for learning through the senses and through the miracle of language and the cognitive abilities to read and write.

When examining the concept of knowingness, we must recognize that various spheres of influence fuel readers' cognitive schema; thus, it follows that each reader's schema is personal. All of us have unique patterns of understanding, connectivity, gaps, and overlaps in our knowledge based on how new information connects with known information, data, and lingering misconceptions. That new knowledge is what our cognitive maps store for us. The goal of knowledge is to connect, slot, and link new information in meaningful ways so that we have the information when we need it.

To revisit and deepen readers' thinking about how learners acknowledge, acquire, and assimilate knowledge is a never-ending journey for educators. The following list describes the kinds of knowledge experiences that teachers can use to help students grow new cognitive connections. This fuels their quest to know by continually seeking, experiencing, and storing incoming inputs. It briefly explains the subtle differences in how the mind-filling miracle of knowledge manifests itself for literate individuals. This does include corresponding vocabulary tiers (NGA & CCSSO, 2010).

- **Prior knowledge (tiers one, two, and three vocabulary):** A personal schema available to receive incoming neural signals; previous learning that scaffolds new learning (patterns of language that accumulate over time, mainly through auditory and visual senses)

  Example: Knowing addition facts helps a student learn subtraction facts.

- **Background knowledge (tiers one and two vocabulary):** Ongoing and experiential incidents that become readily accessible to set the stage for further learning within a known context or frame of understanding; lays the groundwork for using what is relevant in a situation

  Example: When a Girl Scout knows a lot about the woods near her house, she takes that relevant knowledge with her when she goes on a camping trip in a national forest with her troop.

- **Contextual knowledge (tier three vocabulary; knowledge-centric vocabulary):** Knowledge taken from a specific context to understand the gist of an idea; readers derive meaning by reading between the lines and figuring out what knowledge-centric words mean from the clues and cues that come from the actual reading

  Example: When a character in a story is described as "drenched as he puts down his broken umbrella," readers may not know the word *drenched*, yet they can surmise that it was raining hard from the words *broken umbrella*. From their own knowledge of pouring rain, they can pick up the gist of the word *drenched*.

- **Content-specific knowledge (tier two academic vocabulary):** Knowledge that requires deep understanding to connect it to existing knowledge; knowledge derived from a specific context facilitates learning connected content from that first context

  Example: If a student studies plants in a unit on living things, he or she has a leg up when studying the biology of human beings. One singular learning experience can provide a deep-enough understanding that it immediately comes to mind and influences the other situation.

- **Domain-specific knowledge (tier three vocabulary; knowledge-centric vocabulary):** Highly complex, sophisticated, and very obscure knowledge; based on language-specific words not considered common knowledge

  Example: Pharmacists must know the compound complexity, common side effects, and compatibility with other prescriptions for each drug they dispense to clients (such as omeprazole, sodium lauryl sulfate, and titanium dioxide).

Existing knowledge is arranged in our brain in patterns of neural connectivity that are definitely inherent in the brain's workings. Yet with every influx of new inputs, the brain creates strikingly different patterns of knowingness depending on the available sources of information, factual data, hunches, and human intuition that guide the formation of cognitive knowing.

Three-Tiered Vocabulary

Here is a look at the three tiers of commonly adopted vocabulary contained in the CCSS (NGA & CCSSO, 2010). This connection between standards and vocabulary, made intentionally, serves to accentuate the inextricable link between vocabulary words as concepts that become part of our ever-expanding knowledge base.

Tier One Words

- Tier one words are everyday speaking vocabulary—*house, weather, food, play*—that Julia A. Simms and Robert J. Marzano (2019) claim are the most common of the common, everyday words students already know upon arriving at school.

- They are usually learned at home, in the neighborhood, and in the early grades, albeit not at the same rate by all students.

- They are not considered a challenge to the average native speaker, though English learners of any age will have to attend carefully to them.

- While tier one words are important, they are not the focus of this discussion.

Tier Two Words

- Tier two words are general academic vocabulary in written texts.

- They appear in all sorts of texts across the disciplines: informational texts (words such as *relative, vary, formulate, specificity,* and *accumulate*), technical texts (words such as *calibrate, itemize,* and *periphery*), and literary texts (words such as *misfortune, dignified, faltered,* and *unabashedly*).

- Tier two words often represent subtle or precise ways to say relatively simple things—*saunter* instead of *walk*, for example. To use them is to be tuned in to word choice, always seeking the just-right word.

Tier Three Words

- Tier three words are domain-specific vocabulary.

- They are specific to a domain or field of study (words such as *magma, carburetor, legislature, circumference,* and *aorta*) and key to understanding a new concept within a text.

- Tier three words are far more common in informational texts than in literature.

- They are recognized as new and hard words for most readers.

- They are often explicitly defined by the author of a text, repeatedly used, and otherwise heavily scaffolded (for example, they appear in a glossary).

Vocabulary Families

- **High-mileage words:** Clusters that are frequent in one topic area—*baby, bottle,* and *crib*

- **High-mileage word families:** The most common forms—*available, availability,* and *unavailable*

We grow knowledge and continually connect to our ever-expanding schema. This signals that paradoxical thought related to the Matthew effect (Stanovich, 1986): "The more we know, the more we know." And conversely, as the saying goes, "The more we know, the more we know we don't know." Yet there is another critically important component that completes that thought. "The more we know, the more we know, don't know and . . . *the more we want to know*." This alludes to the often-neglected truth that reading is a motivator in itself.

The Motivation of Reading

The more we read, the better we read, and the better we read, the more we read, and the more we know . . . and the dominoes continue to fall. In our experience, students *like* hard stuff. They like challenges. They like stepping up and conquering whatever problem they're given. Do you know why? The reason students welcome real challenge is because it speaks to their sense of self. A challenge tells students, "My teacher believes in me. She thinks I can do this." High expectations motivate (Marzano, 2017). Just ask that great teacher you know, "Do you know if your students believe that you believe in them?" and the response will almost always be *yes*, because they expect students' personal best in effort and results and they say that all of the time.

Reading moves us as it moves into our lives. Let's take a moment to explore the idea of motivation to read. Reading is key to building that hunger to read, to know more, and to ignite the natural curiosity that leads us to the love of reading that often sustains us for a lifetime (Willingham, 2017). Again, the more we read, the more we know, and the more we know, the more we read. This willful desire to read comes not only from the curious need to know but also from the magic and wonder of reading with knowingness.

Motivation to read is critical for developing readers. These students wonder about things; they're curious, and they want to know more. Thus, as educators, we can easily motivate them and hook them on reading. Once we realize the power of the reader versus the nonreader in the classroom, we can provoke and entice students to read using many tools at our disposal. We can show them pictures from books that create a sense of wonder, read to them each day so they can't wait to find out what comes next, design classroom challenges based on the number of books read in the room (like a paper caterpillar that worms its way around the classroom, with each segment representing the title of a book a student had read) . . . and the list could go on. Creating curiosity and the drive to know is also possible through book reports about why students wanted to read their chosen book.

Reading with wonder results from a feeling of amazement and admiration caused by something remarkable or unfamiliar, which ignites emotions that spark readers to go on reading. How do we make reading such a joy for students? How do we inspire students to become eager readers who read in their spare moments, even far into the night under their covers with a flashlight? We can start by keeping in mind the following wonderful results of reading for knowingness.

- **Reading for knowingness informs:** It provides necessary data and facts and is laden with knowledge.

- **Reading for knowingness interests readers:** It compels and pushes them, sparking curiosity.

- **Reading for knowingness reveals insights:** It invites introspection and helps readers reflect on subtle truths.

- **Reading for knowingness enlightens:** It heightens the imagination, invoking the dreamer and lifting the reader.

- **Reading for knowingness reveals relevant connections:** It develops meaningful linkages.

- **Reading for knowingness sustains readers' appetite:** It keeps readers hooked, deterring pauses or stops.

- **Reading for knowingness inspires readers:** It helps them self-ignite with voice and choice as they self-direct and achieve goals.

- **Reading for knowingness intertwines with a school ethos:** It facilitates a culture or climate of knowingness to celebrate reading.

In addition to motivating readers, there are two other, sometimes conflicting arenas that impact the power of reading: (1) content knowledge and (2) wonder.

Content Knowledge Matters

Motivation to read often enters through the doorway of independent reading. Yet motivation to read to learn often follows the path laid out in classroom instructional reading sessions. Education professor and writer David Perkins (1992) offers the following view on the power of knowingness: "Knowledge comes on the coattails of thinking" (p. 8). We take from this that without rich, rigorous, and relevant content, we have little to think about. And, correspondingly, the more thinking we do as we read this content (biology, literature, physics, French history, or health and exercise, for example), the more understanding and insight we will develop about the real meaning and the true essence of this knowledge, and the more we will drive our classroom think tank. This complements our discussion of the Matthew effect (Stanovich, 1986).

As we've established, knowingness is about what we get from reading rather than the process of reading. "What do you know that you didn't know before? What have you learned? What's your takeaway?" These are the metacognitive follow-up questions that take students deeper in their thinking and reflection on the content. If we, as teachers, attend to the results of reading, students will think about the purpose of the reading instead of just considering it a task to finish.

Literacy is a thread that weaves throughout all subject areas. We may not all be teachers of reading, but we are all teachers of literacy with a collective mission to entice students to read about our content. This mission directs us to the literacy curriculum as the massive elephant in the room; the necessity of literacy excellence is always there, regardless of the content or context of the class, regardless of grade level and disciplinary content knowledge.

An age-old story suggests that elementary teachers love their students, secondary teachers love their content, and college professors love themselves. This trope alludes to the content-driven curriculum that most schools teach at the upper levels of K–12 and college. To clarify, knowledge-centric curriculum is not the same as content-driven curriculum. Rather, knowledge-centric classrooms are designed with the attainment of knowledge as a core outcome, whatever the subject matter, grade level, discipline, or department. And to attain that effectively and skillfully, reading, writing, speaking, and listening are critical to the performance products and results that are attained. Though highly departmental curricular configurations often see these essential elements of a knowledge-centric classroom as having lesser importance, to produce fully literate graduates, we must strive for them to advance their literacy excellence in our planning of curriculum and instruction.

Knowledge-centric classrooms rely heavily on a powerful literacy curriculum of reading, writing, speaking, and listening. This rich, relevant, and resounding curriculum begs for a full and robust discussion that addresses the curriculum dilemma occurring in U.S. schools. Imagine a ninth-grade teacher who says, "I don't teach reading and writing. I teach social studies. I want kids to come to this class with their literacy skills mastered and ready to go." But there are still expectations for reading competencies and writing conventions for that social studies teacher and other subject matter staff, and teachers must acknowledge them. So, let's carry on, keeping in mind Vygotsky's (1986) beliefs about how thoughts and words relate as a living process. Reframing literacy requires that we be clear about curriculum, what we expect of students and teachers, and ways to make the now invisible thread of literacy more visible as part of student excellence in their work.

Wonder Matters Just as Much

As noted, motivating developing readers to read is critical. These students wonder about things, they're curious, and they want to know more—thus, they are easily hooked on reading. Wonder and inspiration are the joy of reading, just as content knowledge is often the seed of ideas that grow and blossom.

Part of our mission as educators is to entice students to want to read. Just look at the reason our mission is so urgent and universally accepted: the long, unchanging flatline in reading performances sends the signal, loud and clear. Our students are not up to par in their literacy mastery as evidenced by the flatlining trend discussed previously. We must always make intrinsic motivation to read a priority in the classroom. We must do whatever it takes to present our students with the gift of literacy. The question, of course, is *how* do we do that? We hope that readers, singly or in grade-level or department teams, merge their best ideas into a reframing plan for literacy in their classrooms.

What Baffles Teachers About Curriculum

Traditionally, teachers often feel a distinct lack of ownership over curriculum, as it is often specified by the leadership. Even when encouraged to develop their own ideas by team leaders, they are reluctant to do so. They have the test on their minds at all times. So, it is to be expected that teachers may be baffled about how to pursue a knowledge-centric curriculum after having a content-driven one for most of their careers.

What is it exactly that baffles us about curriculum? Let's take a big-picture look at curriculum. In short, curriculum documents do not make clear, or leaders do not state out loud, that reading is a way of learning about the world. It's how we can acquire knowledge about all sorts of things. While knowledge is honored in many disciplined-based middle and secondary school classes (such as American history and biology), ELA curriculum documents such as the Common Core (NGA & CCSSO, 2010) often fully address a myriad of skills with little reference to specific knowledge-centric content.

That said, curriculum does simmer on the back burner when teacher teams address the concerns of the hour, the day, or the time of year. In spite of the overwhelming thought of approaching changes to curriculum, it is already happening as a result of the COVID-19 school closures. Looking on the bright side, maybe the time is right in the midst of dramatic changes already occurring. During the many team meetings that are no doubt occurring as schools figure out how to fulfill their missions, it would be well worth it to give it some thought and see what happens. We could have the *best* year ever in reading performances . . . even though standardized tests have been widely cancelled.

The Challenges of Implementing a Knowledge-Centric, Knowledge-Rich Curriculum

Many things can work against the implementation of a knowledge-rich curriculum. First, many elementary teachers feel that extensive work with social studies and some aspects of science may be developmentally inappropriate in the early grades. According to Wexler (2019), "Relying on the work of the influential twentieth-century psychologist Jean Piaget, education schools have long trained teachers to believe that historical concepts are simply too abstract for children below third or fourth grade to grasp," and the same goes for "any aspects of science that can't be communicated through simple, hands-on experiments" (Wexler, 2019, p. 16). Wexler (2019) refutes this:

> The fact is, history is a series of stories. And kids love stories. The same is true for science topics that don't lend themselves to hands-on activities. It's ironic that truly abstract concepts like captions [which might be taught as a text feature of nonfiction] and symbols are considered appropriate for six-year-olds, but informational tales about history, science, and the arts are not. (p. 28)

Teachers also challenge the idea of a knowledge-rich curriculum because they are concerned that students would find it boring. Fears of rote memorization and low-level recall abound. But our conversations should not be about *whether* we should more thoughtfully impart knowledge. That is settled; we should, and we must. The most helpful conversations would be about *what* knowledge we should impart to students and *how* we decide. We must keep in mind that students will *not* be bored by anything we do with curriculum that is fresh, fascinating, not well-known, relevant in some way, and open to all—teachers, students, administrators. Knowledge is a powerful motivational tool.

Students could learn about the drafting of the U.S. Constitution through a lecture, and they could also learn about it through a simulation in which they assume the roles of delegates from small and large states trying to decide on representation and seeking a compromise. As noted in *Unlocking Student Talent: The New Science of Developing Expertise*, "While anything can be overdone and we clearly need a balance between working with the basics and then applying them in deep and open-ended ways, spending time focusing on basic facts and operations need not be [so negatively characterized]" (Fogarty, Kerns, & Pete, 2018, p. 69).

Quite ironically, at the same time that U.S. education's emphasis has been anywhere other than on knowledge, seeking to foster critical thinking as the first priority, leading authors and teaching experts Doug Lemov, Erica Woolway, and Katie Yezzi (2012) note that we should not consider facts and information "the enemy of higher-order thinking," as "it's all but impossible to have higher-order thinking without strongly established skills and lots of knowledge of facts" (p. 37). Educationalist Dylan Wiliam (2018) remarks:

> The big mistake we have made in the United States, and indeed in many other countries, is to assume that if we want students to be able to think, then our curriculum should give them lots of practice in thinking. This is a mistake because what our students need is more to think *with*. . . . The only way to make humans more capable in their thinking is to expand the store of things that they have to think with—in other words, to have more knowledge in long-term memory. (pp. 134, 155)

As mentioned previously, in our efforts to raise reading and mathematics scores, we have mistakenly cut time from science and social studies classes—experiences that afford much of the general knowledge required for overall success.

Another impediment to a knowledge-rich curriculum is a lack of specificity in most standards documents, particularly for ELA. While social studies and science standards, by their very nature, are far more specific about content knowledge, ELA standards documents often spend page after page listing skills that students must master. Social studies lists topics like Reconstruction and Ancient Egypt. Science topics might cover force, ecosystems, and waves. Meanwhile, ELA more often leaves the choice of text (the true content) open, and suggests something like comparing and contrasting alternate versions of the same story. Not surprisingly, this creates the impression that teachers' emphasis must be on skills.

How many teachers in states that implement the Common Core even realize that those standards also point out the need to equally consider content and knowledge? The introduction to the Common Core State Standards for ELA clearly states, "The Standards . . . do not—indeed, cannot—enumerate all or even most of the content that students should learn. The Standards must therefore be complemented by a well-developed, content-rich curriculum" (NGA & CCSSO, 2010, p. 6). Teachers must know that the standards represent broad strokes of expectations for the educated person; many schools have not given serious thought to the knowledge aspects of their curriculum yet still feel that they are implementing their state standards that grew from the original CCSS.

Finally, it would be easy to believe that we no longer need to teach students facts because of the 21st century's world of easy information access. Why have students learn about the presidents or state capitals when Google or Siri can provide them via voice command or a few taps of a keyboard? Hirsch (2018) addresses this misguided idea, telling us that looking things up is "a completely unsatisfactory procedure compared to having a well-stocked mind" (Hirsch, 2018, p. 81). In addition, "Psychologists have found that students simply will not read at all if they have to look up too many words" (Willingham, 2008, as cited in Hirsch, 2018, p. 82). Readers need to know, as Willingham stated, about 98 percent of the words to achieve fluency and comprehension. So when students have to repeatedly look up words or facts, either they stop reading altogether because they lack the understanding they need, or they skip over the words and ideas they do not understand, and they find their overall comprehension significantly diminished.

The Meaning of Knowledge-Rich Curriculum

Wiliam (2018) notes, "The word *curriculum* is used in a number of different ways in the United States" and, sadly, "in a much more specific sense to describe the *textbooks* that a district has adopted (as in, 'We changed our curriculum,' meaning 'We changed our textbook')" (p. 121). Is the collective knowledge we really want to impart to students so transitory as to be fundamentally altered by adopting a new textbook? What if someone attempted to outline the knowledge required for someone to be literate?

Someone did just that. With his 1987 book *Cultural Literacy: What Every American Needs to Know*, University of Virginia professor E. D. Hirsch Jr. made an attempt to lay out this knowledge. According to civic engagement advocate Eric Liu (2015), Hirsch's "book was an argument—textured and subtle, not overtly polemical—about why nations need a common cultural vocabulary and why public schools should teach it." But rather than focusing on the work as a whole, many critics focus on the book's appendix, "an unannotated list of about 5,000 names, phrases, dates, and concepts that, in [the view of Hirsch and two collaborators], 'every American needs to know'" (Liu, 2015).

Hirsch was immediately and unfairly "cited by pundits who would never read the book" who felt that this list was "heavy on the deeds and words of the 'dead white males'" (Liu, 2015). Decades later, however, Hirsch's work is experiencing a renaissance of sorts. The context of and research base supporting his idea of a knowledge-rich curriculum are now better understood, and Hirsch's (2018) dream for his knowledge-rich curriculum to be "egalitarian in purpose and result" (p. 160) is beginning to be realized.

We could devote an entire volume to discussing Hirsch's work. Suffice it to say that the research base on the need for knowledge to support reading comprehension is now solid. Also, at a time when the United States is both more diverse and more divided than ever, multiple authors suggest that giving all Americans a consistent knowledge base is a key element to ensure equity of opportunity (Hirsch, 1987; Wexler, 2019; Willingham, 2017). Liu (2015) captures this sentiment:

> The more serious challenge, for Americans new and old, is to make a common culture that's greater than the sum of our increasingly diverse parts. It's not enough for the United States to be a neutral zone where a million little niches of identity might flourish; in order to make our diversity a true asset, Americans need those niches to be able to share a vocabulary. Americans need to be able to have a broad base of common knowledge so that diversity can be most fully activated.

> A generation of hindsight [on Hirsch's work] now enables Americans to see that it is indeed necessary for a nation as far-flung and entropic as the United States, one where rising economic inequality begets worsening civic inequality, *to cultivate continuously a shared cultural core. A vocabulary. A set of shared referents and symbols.* (emphasis added)

By visiting www.coreknowledge.org, educators can access and download, at no cost, a variety of curricular resources for the Core Knowledge approach to ELA, science, and social studies that seriously considers the articulation of the knowledge to be imparted. Hirsch (2018) himself notes that "the Core Knowledge Sequence is put forward only as an example of what such a curriculum looks like in the American context" (p. 159). Use Core Knowledge, or build your own content. These are the options. Whichever option you choose, you must thoughtfully consider the knowledge within your curriculum. Not thoughtfully considering knowledge within curricula does a grave disservice to students.

For schools that choose to use Core Knowledge, it is often wise to add some local elements. To be culturally literate in East Coast states requires knowledge of British colonial history. Spanish colonial history plays more of a role in states like Florida and California. We similarly cannot forget the impact of the French in Louisiana. Texans will remind you that their state was once its own country, and citizens of Oklahoma are surrounded by Native American culture and had best have some understanding of it. Wexler (2019) believes that the United States "is probably too diverse for [a single detailed national curriculum] . . . but there is much we can do" (p. 39). As just noted, Core Knowledge resources give us an excellent beginning on just that, the core. Then, schools could supplement that national core with the previously mentioned local elements.

Potential Pitfalls of Adding to Curriculum

We advocate that schools should add to their curricular documents elements of knowledge that are relevant to their circumstances where these elements are not present. As previously noted, we can spell out the names, dates, places, important people, important events, useful allusions, and key concepts that should be discussed as students make their way through school. For example, given the many common references to elements of Greek mythology, knowledge of the topic has utility. As a result, the curriculum documents for any district could spell out when mythology would best be taught and what topics might be covered. However, adding *anything* to curricula can have two potentially perilous results. One relates to ELA in particular, and the other is relevant to all content areas.

First, as previously noted, other content areas are generally more complete than ELA when it comes to the presence of knowledge in their curricula. For example, science and social studies curriculum documents are focused on very discrete and agreed-on topics, while ELA tends to be a list of skills, with only passing references to potential texts through which to operationalize those skills. For ELA, we need to note that when you choose a book, you are choosing content. If, for example, one chooses to teach a unit on *Lord of the Flies*, one has decided that this particular novel conveys meaningful intellectual capital. Novels, plays, poems, and essays can be viewed as the content knowledge of ELA.

But, as Schmoker (2018) remarks, "English language arts (ELA), more than any other discipline, has lost its way" (p. 115). ELA, more than any other subject area, suffers the most when it comes to balancing both the knowledge and the skills of its content area. So, when attempting to add to ELA documents, we must help teachers feel confident about making room for knowledge by letting go of their very skill-based focus.

The cry, by many, for fewer ELA skills–based standards is ongoing. Stiggins (2017) notes the challenge that "content specialists often struggle to agree on priority standards, and . . . they seem unable to limit the number of standards to be taught" (p. 51). When everything is a priority, nothing is a priority. How do we compress the skills to make room for knowledge? How do we help narrow the skills focus to what matters most?

In lieu of lists of hundreds of language arts skills that many educators do not even truly consult, education policy professor David T. Conley (2005) suggests the following four objectives, which could adequately condense all those skills:

1. Read to infer/interpret/draw conclusions.
2. Support arguments with evidence.
3. Resolve conflicting views encountered in source documents.
4. Solve complex problems with no obvious answer. (as cited in Schmoker, 2018, p. 39)

In a similar attempt, Lemov et al. (2016) distill the Common Core ELA standards into the following four ideas:

1. Read harder texts.
2. "Close read" texts rigorously and intentionally.
3. Read more nonfiction more effectively.
4. Write more effectively in direct response to texts. (p. 5)

Schmoker (2018) suggests that Conley's "short, simple standards would replace the majority of our (so-called) literacy standards" (p. 39). There is a place for references to and a focus on skills, but not a focus on learning skills at the expense of gaining content knowledge. In too many classrooms, teachers are so busy covering all the skills that there is no time left for students to read and write about what they have learned. As we previously noted, skill building has its uses up to a point, but more is not better, while more background knowledge is (Willingham & Lovette, 2014). Skills, as we have established, are commonly overdone, especially in a spiraling, often repetitive curricula, while knowledge is more often spread out over the various grades and disciplines.

Related to this, Lemov et al. (2016) say, "What students read is among the most important considerations a school can address" (p. 54). They further assert, "Text selection deserves greater attention and intentionality. In the ELA classroom, choosing text is choosing knowledge" (Lemov et al., 2016, p. 55). They advise, "One of the most important things you can do to get the most out of text selection is coordinate" (Lemov et al., 2016, p. 52). In short, we should thoughtfully plan for building knowledge, and for bringing the actual activities of reading and writing back to the forefront of our classrooms. If we want a highly literate populace, we must embed these core literacy activities across the curriculum.

This is where the second potentially perilous aspect of adding to curriculum documents comes to light. We have to achieve a fine balance between ensuring consistent experiences for students, regardless of the teacher, and not making teachers feel as if they must follow a rigid script. When two high school students take the same course from two different teachers, they should have relatively similar experiences. For this to happen, we must spell some things out. If, however, we spell things out too much, it becomes paralyzing. No teachers enter the profession to have someone hand them a script. If we specify the content for every single day, it will leave no room for teachable moments or logical connections between content and current world events that arise. Schmoker (2018) presents a way to achieve this balance by spelling out much of the specific content for each course, but also leaving enough room for things like the teacher's interests and passions, the teachable moments that arise, or the unforeseen opportunities to connect the content of a course to current events.

Useful Examples of Curriculum Maps

Figures 3.3 and 3.4 reflect the level of detail Mike Schmoker (2018) feels might be ideal for curriculum documents. Notice that for each week, there is a clear notation of the topic, key resources, and targeted number of days of instruction, which appear in brackets. Then, when applicable, there is a writing prompt. You will also note that the calculus example (figure 3.3) devotes many weeks to content that might take only three to four days to cover. This gives the teacher time to cover topics and make decisions based on his or her professional judgment or in response to teachable moments or current world events. In the language arts example (figure 3.4), the teacher has opportunities to choose additional nonfiction articles and works of literature. Visit **go.SolutionTree.com/literacy** for blank versions of these templates.

Week	Concepts and Topics (Approximate days in brackets)	Textbook Pages and Other Key Resources	Writing Prompts (When applicable)
1	**Unit 1: Limits and their properties** 1.1—A preview of calculus [2] 1.2—Finding limits graphically and numerically [3]	1.1—pp. 57–63 1.2—pp. 65–71	
2	1.2—Finding limits graphically and numerically (continued) 1.3—Evaluating limits analytically [3]	1.2—pp. 65–71 1.3—pp. 76–83	Write to explain the respective advantages of finding limits in the following ways. a. Graphically b. Numerically c. Analytically
3	1.4—Continuity and one-sided limits [3]	Quiz: 1.1–1.3 1.4—pp. 87–95	

4	1.5—Infinite limits [3] 1.6—Limits at infinity [2]	1.5—pp. 100–104 1.6—pp. 108–114	
5	1.6—Limits at infinity (continued)	1.6—pp. 108–114	How are infinite limits different from limits at infinity? Explain in writing.
6	Unit 2: Differentiation 2.1—The derivative and the tangent line problem [3]	Unit 1 test 2.1—pp. 123–130	
7	2.2—Basic differentiation rules and rates of change [4]	2.2—pp. 134–142	
8	2.3—Product and quotient rules and higher-order derivatives [3]	2.3—pp. 147–153	
9	2.4—The chain rule [4]	Quiz: 2.1–2.3 2.4—pp. 158–167	Write to compare and contrast the following. a. Product rule b. Quotient rule c. Chain rule

Total instructional days—year to date: 31 of 132

Source: © 2018 by Mike Schmoker. Adapted with permission.

Figure 3.3: Calculus curriculum document.

*Visit **go.SolutionTree.com/literacy** for a free reproducible version of this figure.*

Texts to Teach in First Marking Period	Text Taught With Embedded Vocabulary Instruction	Guiding Question for Close Reading, Discussion, and Writing
Novel (1)	*Sarah, Plain and Tall* (MacLachlan, 1985)	How do Anna and her relationships change throughout the book? Support your answer with evidence and details from the text. (Two-page paper)

Figure 3.4: Grade 3 ELA curriculum document.

continued ▶

Texts to Teach in First Marking Period	Text Taught With Embedded Vocabulary Instruction	Guiding Question for Close Reading, Discussion, and Writing
Nonfiction book (1)	*The Boy Who Invented TV* (Krull, 2009)	What significant changes did Philo go through? Support your answer with evidence and details from the text. (Two-page paper)
Articles (6–8)	"Veterans Day at 100" from myON News Five to seven additional articles from myON News	Given the history and purpose of Veterans Day, do you feel that our current ways for observing the holiday are appropriate or not? Support your answer with evidence from the text. (One- to two-page paper)
Poetry (6–10 samples)	*The Giving Tree* (Silverstein, 1964)	What are the three important things that the tree gave to the boy? Explain your choices, and give evidence from the book. (One- to two-page paper)
Major writing assignments	The four preceding papers, plus weekly targeted writing instruction and activities	

Source: ©2018 by Mike Schmoker. Adapted with permission.
*Visit **go.SolutionTree.com/literacy** for a free reproducible version of this figure.*

ELA's Eloquent Solution: Pairing Fiction and Nonfiction Texts

As previously noted, Schmoker (2018) says, "English language arts (ELA), more than any other discipline, has lost its way" (p. 115). Misinterpretations of the Common Core's recommendations around the amount of nonfiction reading that students should do don't help. Some mistakenly believe that quality literature's role in the ELA classroom is being significantly diminished. This is not the case, but we do need to discuss how we maintain the central role of literature in ELA and also address the accepted need for our students to become better consumers of nonfiction.

Lemov et al. (2016) note that they "support the idea that students could read more nonfiction, as long as they also continue to read plenty of great fiction"

(p. 121). They observe, however, that "as important as reading *more* nonfiction is, reading nonfiction *more effectively*" is of equal consideration (Lemov et al., 2016, p. 121). Let's explore how we can guide students to read nonfiction more thoughtfully and effectively in ELA classrooms.

Lemov et al. (2016) assert that the ideal solution involves "the synergy between reading nonfiction and fiction" (p. 121). They differentiate texts as primary texts and secondary texts, each of which may be either fiction or nonfiction. *Primary texts*, not to be confused with primary source documents, are the texts "chosen as the principal reading material for a particular class" (Lemov et al., 2016, p. 122). *Secondary texts* are the "additional shorter texts that relate to the primary text in some way" (Lemov et al., 2016, p. 122). They "give context, provide background, show a contrast, or develop a useful idea that helps students better engage [with] the primary text" (Lemov et al., 2016, p. 122).

Lemov and his coauthors (2016) shape their dialogue around a consideration of fostering the best absorption rate—"how quickly students assimilate new knowledge as they read" (p. 121). They believe that when teachers thoughtfully pair texts, "the absorption rate of both texts goes up"; they recommend that teachers consider two types of text pairings, those "inside the bull's-eye" and those "outside the bull's-eye" (Lemov et al., 2016, p. 123).

Inside the Bull's-Eye

In terms of pairing texts, inside-the-bull's-eye pairings are more straightforward and common. They involve "content necessary to support basic understanding of the primary text" (Lemov et al., 2016, p. 123). For example, if *To Kill a Mockingbird* (Lee, 1960) is the primary text, students might read a nonfiction article about Jim Crow laws or the Great Depression as a secondary text. In an ELA classroom, "nonfiction . . . is ideal as a secondary text" (Lemov et al., 2016, p. 122).

Text pairings are all about creating synergy. Lemov et al. (2016) tell of a teacher who paired a nonfiction article on wartime rationing (the secondary text) with *Lily's Crossing* (Giff, 1997), a young-adult novel set during World War II (the primary text). They remark on the synergy of the pairing, noting:

> Students got more out of the secondary text when they could apply it to people they were interested in and felt a connection to—even if they were fictional characters. Students realized that these events really affected the lives of people during World War II—they weren't just mundane, isolated facts in an article. (Lemov et al., 2016, p. 124)

Outside the Bull's-Eye

Outside-the-bull's-eye pairings are a bit harder to conceive and construct. They are more novel and creative. They involve secondary texts that cause students

continued ▶

to "look at the primary text in a new and unexpected or more rigorous way" (Lemov et al., 2016, p. 123).

Lemov et al. (2016) offer an example of a teacher who had her middle school students read *The Outsiders* by S. E. Hinton (1967). She observed that "two hidden themes of the novel were the power of class and caste, and the influence of male bonding" and sought out nonfiction articles related to these ideas (Lemov et al., 2016, p. 126). When she found a *Smithsonian Magazine* article detailing research into "how younger male elephants learn their social behaviors by watching and modeling slightly older peers" (Lemov et al., 2016, p. 126), its connections to the novel were immediately apparent. This creative pairing resulted in synergy and a very creative discussion where she "asked her classes to apply terms like *hierarchy* to *The Outsiders* as well," allowing students to "find evidence that the social structures of the Greasers and Socs weren't necessarily unique to humans, but were actually similar to those of the rest of the animal kingdom" (Lemov et al., 2016, p. 126).

While inside-the-bull's-eye pairings "make the unfamiliar familiar," outside-the-bull's-eye pairings can make "the familiar more rigorous" in unique ways (Lemov et al., 2016, pp. 126–127).

Reading Success Through Text Sets

Coming to understand the critical role of background knowledge in reading comprehension sheds new light on why teachers might choose to use text sets—multiple texts on the same topic—with students. As teacher and writer Shannon Garrison (2016) notes, *text sets* are "collections of texts tightly focused on a specific topic," which, despite the name, "may include varied genres (fiction, nonfiction, poetry, and so forth) and media (such as blogs, maps, photographs, art, primary-source documents, and audio recordings)." They can vary rather significantly in form and purpose. For example, "some are arranged as series of texts (and other media) that become progressively more advanced," while others assign more primacy to "a central or 'anchor' text with supplementary texts that support the themes and content of the central text" (Garrison, 2016). Differences in purposes acknowledged, Garrison (2016) feels that "all high-quality text sets are designed to build knowledge of an academic topic" and "are presented in a specific order with attention to text complexity, vocabulary development, content knowledge, and conceptual understanding."

For our purposes here, we would like to highlight the use of text sets with struggling readers. As with all text sets, the focus on a particular topic is key, but in this situation, teachers must place particular emphasis on arranging the texts in a carefully crafted order of increasing difficulty.

Imagine that you are supporting a struggling seventh-grade student who must be prepared to read and interact with an on-grade-level text on Christopher Columbus. Per the Common Core's quantitative measures of text complexity, this would equate to a text written from 7.0 to 9.9 using an ATOS measure or from 925 to 1185 using a Lexile measure. But the student you are supporting reads at a second-grade level. Assuming that your student does not already possess extensive knowledge of Columbus, reading the on-grade-level text will be exceedingly difficult, because of both the text complexity and the lack of prior knowledge.

We learned earlier, however, that "knowledge of a content domain is a powerful determinant of the amount and quality of information recalled, powerful enough for poor readers to compensate for their generally low reading ability" (Recht & Leslie, 1988, p. 19). So, if you can build up the student's knowledge of the topic, there is a greatly improved chance of success. Text sets can accomplish this. You could begin with texts well within the student's ability (for example, something written about Columbus at an ATOS level of 3.0) and then gradually help the student make it through successively more difficult texts. Each text adds more knowledge, and because the texts revolve around a common topic, Columbus, the knowledge learned from each text gives the student a running start into the next, more difficult one.

Literacy professor and researcher Gay Ivey (2002) notes that the use of text sets results in a dynamic where "the focus of study becomes concepts rather than the content of one particular book. Students gain both a broad perspective and an in-depth sense of the subject matter from reading many texts on the same topic." At this point, gaining knowledge becomes exciting. Hirsch (2018) remarks, "Children are intensely interested in grown-up knowledge. They feel empowered by it, and they are" (p. 163). Additionally, Cervetti et al. (2016) find multiple positive effects when students read conceptually coherent texts, including better retention of concepts and vocabulary.

Writing: The Litmus Paper of Thought

A common theme you see across curriculum maps is writing wherever applicable. Writing is the integral complement to reading on the literacy stage. While we have primarily dealt with the role of reading in literacy acquisition thus far, it is now time that we address the role of writing, which education reformer Ted Sizer describes as "the litmus paper of thought" (as cited in Schmoker, 2006, p. 61). Schmoker (2006) asserts that "we also tend to underestimate how important writing is to intellectual development and career success" (p. 62) while English and education professor Gerald Graff (2003) observes, "Every profession rewards those who are highly competent at devising examples that exemplify one's point [and] generalizing one's conclusions"— skills that writing hones (as cited in Schmoker, 2006, p. 62).

Writing about something we have read about is often a good way to discover that we don't understand that thing as thoroughly as we thought. English professor Lisa Ede (1987) remarks, "Until we attempt to write what we learn or read, our thoughts will lack the precision, depth, and clarity that mark first-rate thinking" (as cited in Schmoker, 2006, p. 65). So, if we want these things for our students—"first-rate thinking" marked by precision, clarity, and depth—we must have them write about what they have read.

Source: © Mark Anderson, www.andertoons.com. Used with permission.

Schmoker (2006) advances that "writing may very well exercise the critical faculties in a way that can't be matched" (p. 63) and Dennis Sparks (2005), former director of Learning Forward, frames writing as "a way of freezing our thinking, or slowing down the thoughts that pass through our consciousness at lightning speed, so that we can examine our views and alter them if appropriate" (as cited in Schmoker, 2006, p. 63). Wexler (2019) simply advises, "If you wanted to enable students to understand what they were reading, convert information into long-lasting knowledge, and learn to think critically, teaching them to write [is] about the best thing you could do" (p. 219).

Additionally, writing can address the concern some might have that emphasizing knowledge would simply result in memorization. Wexler (2019) frames it this way:

> If we want to prevent the rote memorization many teachers fear will result from a focus on knowledge, our best strategy is to explicitly teach students to write about what they're learning. . . . It can serve as a powerful means of pushing students to review facts they've been taught, make connections, and think about them analytically. (pp. 39–40)

Wexler (2019) cautions us, however, not to do with writing what many of us have done with reading, lamenting, "To the extent that writing is included in the curriculum at all, it's taught, like reading comprehension, *in isolation from content*—as though it, too, consisted of a set of free-floating skills" (p. 40, emphasis added). For example, teachers often ask students to write pieces that are personal narratives. They do not facilitate deeper thinking and, because they do not require knowledge but merely personal experience, they do not afford the opportunity for students to refine their understanding of knowledge through writing or to engage more deeply with texts by citing evidence in response to open-ended questions. We might compare a prompt like "My Biggest Surprise" to an evidence-based science prompt like "After reading about motion and force, find the most surprising part of the pendulum experiment, and write with specifics about what happened and why you think it happened." What we want is the synergy that we can achieve by closely tying writing to reading. Schmoker (2006) says, "For all our talk about the importance of higher-order thinking, we continue to overlook the fact that writing, linked to close reading, is the workshop of thought—with an almost miraculous effect on students' critical capacities" (p. 64).

Schmoker (2006) says, "For all our talk about the importance of higher-order thinking, we continue to overlook the fact that writing, linked to close reading, is the workshop of thought—with an almost miraculous effect on students' critical capacities" (p. 64).

The ideal vehicle to reach this dynamic workshop of thought, created by closely tied writing and readings, is having students write responses to open-ended questions that require evidence from the texts they have read. This forces rereading, and editor Deborah Perkins-Gough (2002) has found that "rereading with a purpose is perhaps the most vital strategy for promoting both fluency and deep understanding of texts in every discipline" (as cited in Schmoker, 2006, p. 60).

The reading-writing relationship, if thoughtfully established in literacy acquisition, can be powerfully symbiotic. To fully optimize literacy acquisition, reading needs writing, and writing needs reading. This idea is reflected in two of the six principles of *The Writing Revolution*, where authors Judith C. Hochman and Natalie Wexler (2017) note, "When embedded in the content of the curriculum, writing instruction is a powerful teaching tool. The content of the curriculum drives the rigor of the writing activities" (p. 8).

They expressly state that "writing and content knowledge are intimately related" and that "having students write about topics unrelated to content represents a huge wasted opportunity" because "writing isn't merely a skill; it's also a powerful teaching tool" (Hochman & Wexler, 2017, p. 11). Writing forces students to "synthesize information and produce their own interpretations," helping them ultimately "absorb and retain the substance of what they're writing about and the vocabulary that goes

"When embedded in the content of the curriculum, writing instruction is a powerful teaching tool. The content of the curriculum drives the rigor of the writing activities" (Hochman & Wexler, 2017, p. 8).

with it" (Hochman & Wexler, 2017, p. 11). This seems to echo Schmoker's (2018) earlier declaration: "After one has learned the mechanics of reading, growth depends, more than anything, on our ability to build up students' knowledge base and vocabulary" (p. 27).

Knowledge: A Quick Review

Before we dive into some dynamic knowledge-based classroom applications, let's review. The knowingness of literacy is knowledge—prior knowledge, background knowledge, emergent knowledge, revised knowledge, and knowledge we don't yet know but will invent. Our end goal with the essential components in a curriculum of the knowingness of literacy is to produce aspiring and literate humans—knowing, articulate, and forthcoming individuals who speak and write with authority, regardless of age or experience.

It's no mystery that a knowledge-centric, knowledge-rich, knowledge-driven curriculum should be at the heart of what students talk about, hear about, read about, write about, and think about throughout the school day. Yes, knowledge *is* critical. Yet this central focus on knowledge, in terms of time given or delegated to honing student knowledge, deepening and broadening it for appropriate uses, is not currently where it needs to be. Skill-driven agendas eat up hours of the instructional day, when manipulating new knowledge could be so much more motivating.

This view, based on the most recent findings that we present in this book, accepts that knowledge is the critical center of the educated graduate. And even though knowledge must take precedence over skill development in the curriculum schema, these are the skills of learning that are also important and shouldn't be ignored by teachers. These are the essential skills of reading, writing, speaking, listening, thinking, reasoning, and organizing. These are the skills that expose students to the deeper understanding needed for authentic application and transfer of the joys and anguish of the learning curve in domain-specific content.

To successfully make knowledge the anchor to learning, it is essential that we, as educators, study how the sound, the look, and the knowingness of reading instruction impact student literacy throughout their learning years. That said, let's turn to classroom scenarios to see what literacy reframed looks like for the knowingness of learning. As with the previous chapters, we'll discuss classroom scenarios for grades preK–3, 4–6, 7–8, and 9–12.

These classroom scenarios feature instruction for guided practice and for subsequent student performances that illustrate evidence of learning. Teachers can use these options in their respective classrooms, tailoring them to fit the class and the content. The scenarios model shifts that are sometimes subtle and sometimes not so subtle as they highlight content as a motivational factor. Students reach understanding through the application of keen literacy skills. Our focus on reframing literacy with compelling content helps diminish the time-honored daily schedule that overwhelms students with overskillification. For the bulk of the time in a knowledge-centric classroom, students engage with authentic reading, writing, speaking, and listening opportunities that afford them the critical development necessary to succeed in jobs, college, and careers.

We include strategies for reading to K–12 students. We also supplant the laser focus on skill-and-drill exercises with *reach and repeat* and *deliberate practice*, influenced by our findings that these practices help students sharpen their reading minds, reflect, and hold metacognitive conversations (Fogarty et al., 2018). These innovations can extend specific lessons for a lifetime. In addition, we acknowledge the dire need for explicit instruction in the digital reading domain, as well as encourage hybrid models of digital and print at all levels—and, as always, accountability measures for student reading abilities, motivation, and lifelong literacy habits. These measures (such as anecdotal evidence, criterion-referenced assessments, and normed tests) will show that the proof is in the pudding.

Exploring why, what, when, where, how, and who human beings read is the quintessential journey of the literate world. How would you answer any one of those questions? It may say a whole lot about you. For example, one person might answer the question, "Who wrote it?" She has read libraries full of books. Another person answers the question, "What do I want to read about?" He is quite an eclectic reader. On the other hand, still another person answers the question, "Where will I read about?" He travels widely and tends to read locally and culturally; he can read anywhere, anytime, and any way. Let's find out more about how readers choose their reading material.

Classroom Applications for Teachers

Knowledge-centric classrooms are the very heart and soul of *Literacy Reframed*. More specifically, this refers to the growing knowledge core that builds background knowledge as a catalyst for developing literacy excellence. That's why educators, no matter what level their students are or what content they teach, must fully support and foster the sound, the look, and the knowingness of reading instruction and how to impact student literacy throughout the learning years.

Mrs. Parks's Second-Grade Class

PreK–3's focus is a toolbox of picture-rich visuals that accompany new knowledge and phonics as teachers unlock letter-sound relationships to start students on the path to word knowledge. For the sake of time, the lesson occurs in two parts.

Session 1: Picture Words

This knowledge-building activity is extrapolated from language arts teaching expert Emily F. Calhoun's (1999) Picture Word Inductive Model (PWIM) for students in the early phases of learning literacy who respond positively to it. Mrs. Parks displays a picture of a neighborhood scene for a unit on community. It has a plethora of detailed objects: houses, cars, bikes, doors, trees, sidewalks, windows, people, and so on. She instructs her students to look closely at the displayed picture and name the objects. As they call out the words at random, Mrs. Parks labels each item named. Because students are viewing pictures related to the knowledge-based content they are studying, they are developing their schema within a framework that will pay dividends at the next level.

PWIM is a classic teaching strategy that any teacher could copy just as we've described it. Of course, the discussion will change as the picture changes, but the sense of discovery will always be there for students as they gain confidence in their knowledge of words. That sense of discovery is where the value lies.

To customize this strategy, the teacher might show a picture that features many numbers, such as street addresses, license plates, baseball jerseys, and so on. Instead of looking for objects to identify, students find numbers to read and pronounce correctly. PWIM could also be useful in a foreign language class. Students identify objects in the picture that they believe they can name and pronounce in the language they are studying, and the teacher and fellow students serve as their audience.

Session 2: Sentences to Story

Using the PWIM exercise on developing background knowledge by spotting context clues in the picture, Mrs. Parks has students form sentences about what they know about the words they have provided from the Picture Words session. Then she uses these words to form simple sentences on chart paper. After writing down three to four sentences, Mrs. Parks reads the chart with a storytelling voice. She ends the activity by leading a brief discussion that emphasizes key points about how images and sounds connect as the components of storytelling.

A natural extension of PWIM, this activity takes students from simply identifying words to using the words in sentences. As the students expand their vocabulary, their sentence construction will become more elaborate and hence might take more time. In this case, a teacher may customize the strategy by having the students work in pairs.

Working and sharing accountability for learning with a partner can be a rehearsal for mastery (Schmoker, 2018). As the partners embrace shared accountability (that is, they contribute equally to their conversation), they activate multiple areas of their brains associated with reading, including Broca's area and Wernicke's area (National Aphasia Association, n.d.a, n.d.b). The teacher's role here is critical in ensuring that conversations remain equally distributed. Another advantage of this environment of talking, reading, thinking, sharing, and learning is that it exposes students at an early age to the idea that while they are in school, they are active, not passive, participants in their own learning.

To customize the Sentences to Story strategy beyond the early grades, a teacher can have students look at more complex, historical pictures (such as the painting "Washington Crossing the Delaware"; Leutze, 1851). The teacher would then ask students to not only recognize objects but also identify significant people, places, and things in the picture and then provide more information about what's not in the picture—that is, aspects of the illustrated historical event that the picture does not include.

Miss Hernandez's Fourth-Grade Science Class

Upper-elementary levels are consumed with ongoing reading and writing assignments as well as the development of students' speaking and listening abilities for independent performances. Miss Hernandez uses KWL Posters and Comic Strips to meet these goals.

Session 1: KWL Poster

As part of her earth science unit, Miss Hernandez uses a two-part activity on climate change over two class periods. She starts with Know, Want to Know, Learn (KWL) posters to teach her students current and emerging content knowledge about the phenomenon of climate change. Professor of education Donna Ogle (1986) created the KWL chart, a simple, three-column graphic organizer, as a powerful way to help develop active reading.

Miss Hernandez posts one blank KWL chart for each of six climate change–related topics, and then student groups roll a die to designate which group will work on which topic.

1. Raging fires

2. Violent, massive hurricanes

3. Random tornadoes

4. Prolonged droughts

5. Rising ocean levels

6. Population displacement

Students go to their group's designated KWL poster. As Miss Hernandez monitors the student groups, they add ideas to each of their poster's three columns, listing the following.

1. **What We Know:** Students write down knowledge and facts that they already know about the topic.

2. **What We Want to Know:** Students write down questions about what they want to know about the topic.

3. **What We Learned:** Students record what they learned or what needs to be completed following the Comic Strip presentations on climate change (see session 2).

A teacher can customize the KWL strategy by taping the posters all around the room and having the student groups fill in their What We Know column and then rotate to the next group's poster. Then the groups check to see whether they have anything to add to this poster's What We Know column, they fill in the What We Want to Know column, and they rotate one more time. In this way, the cooperative groups collaborate, and the whole class shares its knowledge in an authentic and student-centered way.

A creative way to transfer the KWL activity focuses on social-emotional learning. In this variation, students do KWL charts on each other. Working in pairs, they discuss what they knew about each other before class started this year, what they want to know about each other, and what they have learned about each other. This conversation relies on students' being both empathic and self-aware.

Session 2: Comic Strip

All groups take the rest of the class period to study their topics. They brainstorm ideas for the next class period, when they will create a five- to six-panel comic strip that delivers a message about what they have learned about their climate change topic. Each comic strip should include at least three facts the students have learned; it must have a distinct point of view, and it must deliver a message that everyone in the group agrees on and can defend.

Student groups each take the following steps to create their comic strip using presentation software like PowerPoint.

1. Students hold an oral discussion to brainstorm ideas.

2. They develop an outline of what they want to say and show.

3. They design a comic strip character with a clever, comical name.

4. They make storyboard sketches to plot the action.

5. They add speech bubbles to the panels.

6. They create an overall title for the comic strip, as well as a name for the specific episode they are featuring.

Finally, the cooperative groups return to their KWL chart and fill in the What We Have Learned column, and Miss Hernandez uploads the final comic strips to the class website. While the idea of students brainstorming and creating a five- to six-panel comic strip in two class periods may seem daunting, we have seen in our own experience that when challenged with creative, open-ended assignments, students will rise to the occasion.

Teachers could customize the Comic Strip activity by asking students to individually write and hand in a position paper using the research their groups uncover, instead of creating a comic strip as a group. In this way, there is cooperative learning but also individual accountability. At the end of the assignment, the group members would still return to their KWL chart to record what they learned. Remember the words of Lisa Ede (1987): "Until we attempt to write what we learn or read, our thoughts will lack the precision, depth, and clarity that mark first-rate thinking" (as cited in Schmoker, 2006, p. 65).

Mr. Ward's Eighth-Grade Health Class

Eighth-grade students are maturing in literacy-laden learning that crosses all disciplines as they become seasoned readers and writers of narrative and informational content. Mr. Ward uses two activities than span two sessions: (1) ABC Graffiti and (2) Interactive Reading.

Session 1: ABC Graffiti

This powerfully motivating prior-knowledge activity invites participation by middle schoolers who have some inkling about the addressed topic. Mr. Ward uses this activity to teach the topic of contagious diseases as part of a unit called "Infectious Diseases: Causes, Contagion, Cures." Most students have limited background knowledge (from childhood cases and personal experiences, teen sex-education classes, and word-of-mouth knowledge) that is just waiting to be developed.

The goal of the ABC Graffiti lesson is to have students gather words related to the topic of contagious diseases. After students get into groups of three to five, Mr. Ward piques their curiosity by targeting their prior knowledge with a brainstorming session. The students try to collect at least one word per letter during this initial brainstorm. Then, Mr. Ward instructs the students to search online for more words to fill in missing letters. This is an opportunity for them to explore the origins and consequences of this important health issue. Their end goal is to create a poster to display their words.

Students within their groups take on various roles.

- **Recorder:** This student needs a marker and chart paper to create the ABC poster (figure 3.5).

- **Researcher:** This student or (students) needs an internet-enabled device. The researcher takes the lead on performing online searches to complete the poster, but anyone in the group can help search.

- **Reporter:** This student needs to report any new words or findings the group uncovered that the group members did not know.

Infectious Diseases: Causes, Contagion, Cures	
A: Airborne	N
B	O
C: COVID-19, coronavirus	P
D	Q
E	R
F	S
G	T: Temperature
H	U
I	V
J	W
K	X
L	Y
M	Z

Figure 3.5: ABC poster template.

Mr. Ward then leads a class discussion to further engage students with the meanings of scientific words. This develops their word knowledge and further cements the new background knowledge they have acquired.

A teacher doing a unit on infectious diseases could easily copy the ABC Graffiti strategy as described. Meanwhile, the possibilities for customization are endless. Teachers from any content area could use this activity with a topic of their choosing: the American Revolution, *To Kill a Mockingbird*, algebra, and so on.

One variation is to do the ABC Graffiti activity before a unit begins and then keep the posters on the classroom walls so they act as word walls that organically fill up as the unit's content unfolds. Or, instead of using the alphabet as the organizing factor, the activity can use a phrase from the unit's content, such as "Declaration of Independence" for American history or "law of conservation of energy" for physics.

Session 2: Interactive Reading

Mr. Ward uploads multiple digital articles and resources related to infectious diseases onto the class website. He tells the students that they have two days to read interactively as they annotate three articles. Each student has to post an original comment on each of the three articles chosen, as well as responding to three different classmate comments. This activity covers three out of the four key objectives that Conley (2005) condenses ELA standards to: (1) read to infer, (2) support arguments with evidence, and (3) resolve conflicting views from sources.

Reading is born of listening and speaking; therefore, reading is a conversation. Online annotating makes this conversation more dynamic than it could ever be in a traditional print environment. This innovation to the traditional process of sharing class notes is possible in the 21st century classroom because technology enables whole classes to share what they have learned in one place. Also, because internet comments identify each commenter along with a time stamp, both summative grading and formative grading are manageable.

There are many ways to customize this online annotation lesson. Whereas the preceding example features multiple resources to read and comment on, teachers who are just beginning to explore the idea of online annotation might post just one brief article. They might scaffold the strategy even more by numbering the paragraphs so the students will be able to easily identify what part of the reading they are referring to when they comment.

A creative transfer of the strategy involves creating a video chat room with an app or online program such as Google Hangouts (http://hangouts.google.com) where students discuss the comments they have posted. In other words, the teacher moves a classroom debate online. The rules for this require that students must cite their sources as they make their points.

Miss Evans's Tenth-Grade Astronomy Class

Secondary students glean critical, evidence-based interpretations in reading, writing, speaking, and listening in all high-level academic matters. They seek clear understanding and success using multiple measures as they prepare for the test of life. A second session follows, which students need to do some work on their own to prepare for.

Session 1: Where's Pluto?

First, Miss Evans assigns students to read two print articles about the discovery of the planet Pluto prior to class. Then, she asks them to read two digital pieces about Pluto's demotion from planethood.

Session 2: Present Your Findings

For the next part of the activity, Miss Evans has students write a two-paragraph essay that compares and contrasts the two processes of discovery and demotion. She directs them to add their personal thoughts on the matter. The students reflect on the two types of reading materials they used for the activity, print and digital, and compare and contrast them in terms of their impact on comprehension.

To customize this lesson, a teacher could simply change the resources that the students are required to read. But, of course, the teacher would still assign reading in two media, print and digital, and have the students compare and contrast them.

In a creative application of this lesson, students would watch and listen to a video of a famous speech and also read the text of the speech. Then the students would compare and contrast the two media, video and print, but they would also compare two different literacy skills: (1) reading and (2) listening.

Bonus: Mrs. Hill's Ninth-Grade World History Class—Critical Thinking With a Capital C

In these days of massive media assaulting student sensibilities from multiple avenues, twenty-four hours a day, seven days a week, Mrs. Hill gives her class a homework reading assignment from a digital article titled "A Beginner's Guide to the French Revolution" (Wilde, 2019). She directs students to report to class ready to do any of three things.

1. Prepare in class a two-paragraph written analysis of the article assigned to them.

2. Prepare an annotated analysis of the article using a digital annotation tool.

3. Prepare and deliver a three-minute speech that compares three specific aspects of the French Revolution to three specific aspects of the American Revolution.

When the students report to class, Mrs. Hill divides them up at random into groups. For example, she says students born between January and April will do the two-paragraph written analysis, those born between May and August will do an annotated analysis, and those born between September and December will prepare three aspects that compare the French Revolution to the American Revolution.

This simple variation of a pretty standard homework assignment captures the attention of the ninth graders, who face the challenge of reading an article but not knowing exactly what they will have to do with the knowledge learned. This uncertainty about which of the three assignments they will have to accomplish heightens their attention and hopefully helps them be cognizant of the mental process that readers go through when considering what they are reading and what they are truly comprehending.

A teacher could customize this lesson by changing either the resource that students have to read or the product the students have to produce to demonstrate mastery. For example, the teacher could give students a reading assignment of a chapter in their history book and tell them to be ready to do one of the three things the next day.

As a variation, the teacher might tell students that they can choose which of the three assignments they will do when they arrive in class the next day, but they won't know exactly what the assignment possibilities will be until it's time to choose. The key aspect of this type of assignment is the engagement level the students demonstrate due to the uncertainty around what they will be expected to do the next day. This level of complexity mirrors key elements of the kinds of problems these students will have to face in their very near future.

Another creative transfer of this lesson would have the students working in pairs, challenging their classmates by coming up with imaginative ways to represent what they learned from the previous night's reading assignment.

PLC Discussion Questions

We provide these discussion questions for use within department or grade-level teams. If your school functions as a professional learning community, these questions are an effective way to encourage professional dialogue in your collaborative team. Conversations like this are key to building trust within the team and helping team members learn from one another. Choose one or several based on interest and concerns exposed during a book study or independent reading of this book.

- Consider the following quote and, with your colleagues, determine which students this quote could pertain to: "A student can be an excellent reader about dinosaurs and a terrible reader about mushrooms" (Hirsch, 2018, p. 75).

- What are three things members of your collaborative team could do tomorrow to reframe the acquisition of knowledge?

- Review the list of knowledge experiences and cognitive schemata on page 97. What kind of knowledge do your students bring to school with them?

What kind of knowledge do students lack and therefore need instruction on?

- How do you motivate your students to read? With your collaborative team, generate a bank of best practices for reading motivation.

- What is more clearly stated in your school—what to teach or how to teach? Explain your reasoning.

- After reading about the importance of core knowledge in literacy instruction, how will you change the way you answer the critical question, "What do we expect our students to learn?" (DuFour et al., 2016).

- How do text sets fit into the principles of differentiation and personalized learning?

- After reviewing the following synthesis of the Common Core ELA standards, decide as a collaborative team which of the listed elements your staff do a good job teaching:

    a. Read harder texts.
    b. "Close read" texts rigorously and intentionally.
    c. Read more nonfiction more effectively.
    d. Write more effectively in direct response to texts. (Lemov et al., 2016, p. 5)

- After reading *Literacy Reframed*, decide as a collaborative team which of the following elements your staff do a good job incorporating into teaching.

    - Reading paired texts (such as one fiction book and one nonfiction book on the same topic, era, or idea)
    - Providing large blocks of time for reading
    - Providing large blocks of time for writing
    - Delivering explicit instruction in effective digital reading
    - Structuring and sequencing phonics programs
    - Emphasizing implicit vocabulary learning
    - Reading often to students at all levels and in all disciplines
    - Fostering reading annotation
    - Reading between the lines by writing between the lines
    - Balancing print and digital reading
    - Planning rich, relevant, robust, riveting content knowledge
    - Using knowledge and knowingness to motivate lifelong literacy

Resources for Learning More

The Writing Revolution by Hochman and Wexler (2017) is an excellent resource. Full of specific strategies and activities, it helps readers move beyond merely assigning writing to understanding far better how to explicitly teach writing.

Other outstanding books in this area include *Why Knowledge Matters* by E. D. Hirsch (2018) and *The Knowledge Gap* by Natalie Wexler (2019).

Downloadable curriculum resources available from www.coreknowledge.org and the Knowledge Matters Campaign (www.knowledgematterscampaign.org) provide a wide variety of resources and support.

CHAPTER 4

Digital Reading

Books are no more threatened by Kindle than stairs by elevators.

—Stephen Fry

We begin with a tale of discovering the hidden miracle of learning to read. Argentine-Canadian novelist and essayist Alberto Manguel (1997) describes a bright, crisp day in 384 AD when the philosopher Augustine (later to be known as Saint Augustine) traveled to Milan to see his teacher, Ambrose. When Augustine arrived, he was perplexed as he saw his revered teacher, seemingly engrossed in a book yet without uttering a word. Unaware that he was witnessing a change in reading behavior that would transform human consciousness, Augustine studied his teacher intently. Ambrose was reading silently, and in doing so, he established an "unrestricted relationship with the book and the words. The words no longer needed to occupy the time required to pronounce them. They could exist in . . . the reader's thoughts" (Manguel, 1997, as cited in La Farge, 2016). Ambrose exhibited a new form of literacy.

Just as Augustine was amazed to see Ambrose reading silently, it would amaze someone from the early 20th century to watch today's readers swipe a digital page of text. Innovations—paper, the printing press, e-readers—have transformed literacy, and they have also tended to generate a range of emotions, from skepticism to enthusiasm, from awe to anguish.

Upon the advent of paper, Socrates feared his instructional method of questions and discussion would be at risk as students moved to private, less formal, and perhaps less well-thought-out means of communication (Nicholas Allard, as cited in Gore, 1998). He thought paper would silence debate, reducing questioning to simple attempts to gain insight of little value. Obviously, there was no cause for alarm. Socrates's personalized interactions and extensive public discourse remained alive, well, and relevant after the technology of paper fully took hold.

Even in our modern world of smart devices and LED lights, older technologies thrive. We still buy paper, pencils, and candles. We still send special-occasion cards through the postal service. Although digital texts are cheaper to access, we, at times, prefer the "feel of a book or a physical newspaper to swiping a screen" (Harford, 2017). We read aloud, often while alone, just to say the words so we absorb them. We read aloud to our children, our students, and our loved ones because doing so builds vocabulary, develops background knowledge, deepens empathy, models expressive reading (*prosody*), and strengthens human relationships. Technologies and humans endure.

On some level, some people may be a bit fearful about how digital texts are transforming reading for their children, worrying that reading will go from a thoughtful experience to one filled with distractions and shallow comprehension. Reading them is so much different than reading text on a page. How do teachers or parents know what books their children are reading as they look at their screens? This connects the dynamics of digital reading with the idea that teachers and parents may lose control of the learning. Others are more curious than fearful in the presence of change. We often fear the unknown, and that is completely natural. So the challenge is to accept that, while change is inevitable, we have a choice in how we will manage it.

Augustine, as far as Manguel (1997) tells us, did not approach Ambrose's inexplicable silent reading—something Augustine had not previously witnessed—with fear; rather, he approached it with curiosity. And according to Manguel (1997), by the 10th century, silent reading, like paper, made human engagement in reading richer. Just as the development of paper or Johannes Gutenberg's printing press marked a change in literacy, digital reading is another shift we will navigate.

The Look and Feel of a Book

The sentiment of Carl Sagan's quote, "What an astonishing thing a book is. It's a flat object made from a tree with flexible parts on which are imprinted lots of funny dark squiggles. But one glance at it and you're inside the mind of another person" (Sagan, Druyan, & Soter, 1980), may capture the essence of a book. Any avid reader knows that the look of reading involves an aesthetic experience that draws one into the book itself. It might include the cover image or color, the title font, or even the smell or texture of the book. The aesthetic pleasure sometimes begins with the search for the book and the tactile act of simply holding the book. Emotions play a part, too, like the joy one can feel when loaning a book to a friend. In fact, even the anticipation of the wait for a specific public library copy to become available can be a pleasure. Those who approach reading as a more casual endeavor may not share a passion for all these aspects of physical books and reading, but theirs is still a tactile memory. Perhaps, it's this sensory experience we miss when we read on an e-reader or tablet as our eyes move across the screen. Sometimes you might hold your Kindle or iPad the same way you hold a bound book, and even though it is a digital device, you can buy a case for it that makes it resemble an actual paper book.

Screenagers (Gen Z, or people in their teens or early twenties who have an aptitude for computers and the internet ["Screenager," n.d.]) have a well-known passion for digital devices of every kind, but older generations are fast catching up and may even surpass younger generations in digital device use (Hoffower, 2019). And this proportion extends to reading for pleasure as well; research shows that older generations read ebooks at least as much if not more than younger generations (Rea, 2020). But across the generations, reading preferences overall tend to print rather than digital books. The look and feel of a book are indeed powerful; in fact, younger generations tend to say that their biggest reason for choosing print books is the feel of the book (Rea, 2020).

Still, digital reading is the preference of many, including those across generations who regularly read in multiple formats (Rea, 2020). Digital tools act as a constant reminder of the unending opportunities to connect with people, words, ideas, and controversies. The appeal of screen time is fueled by the convenience of downloading various reading choices onto one device, the ease of controlling the font size and lighting, and the flexibility of following different threads, meandering off the original subject, and smoothly moving to another like a visual bird walk (Rea, 2020).

Digital literacy and information processing in an electronic environment are also at a premium in the 21st century workplace (Weiss, 2017). The 21st century digital skills of processing technical information, communication, collaboration, critical thinking, creativity, and problem-solving skills are not generally occurring in a print environment (van Laar, van Deursen, van Dijk, & de Haan, 2020). Preparing students for this future is the logical objective of all literacy instruction.

Digital Is Decided

Whether we realize it or not, like paper and silent reading, digital is decided. It is the way of the future, led by school and business communities as they manage all of the many clerical tasks that digital tools handle so expertly.

Just as we always have, we read in libraries, in coffee shops, on trains, and on airplanes. We read at home, in offices, at the beach, and in the park. We read leatherbound, hardbound, or paperback books that have been with us for some time, but now we also read digital books. We leaf through the paper versions or swipe through digital forms of newspapers and magazines. We scroll through online content; the word *scroll* itself evokes the ancient medium upon which our ancestors wrote their texts. We physically manipulate print—turning pages, highlighting key phrases, writing in the margins, applying sticky notes to pages we want to return to later—to find meaning among the words. We read not because we are innately destined to do so but because we are intrinsically driven to imagine stories and understand the world around us. Texts may be taking new forms, but the core of literacy, creating meaning from symbols, remains steadfast in its proper place for readers who are destined to learn through oral language and storytelling, podcasts and videos, but also, through the written word, now sometimes in digital form.

**"You would not believe the battery life on this thing.
I've been reading it for weeks!"**

Source: © *Mark Anderson, www.andertoons.com. Used with permission.*

This transition from printed books to new forms of texts has been decided for some time—it just took a while to achieve scale because human imagination far outpaced the ability to invent practical and reproducible reading technologies. In 1930, Bob Brown (1930/2015), author and cultural critic, lamented that the written word, "bottled up in books" (p. 28), had not kept up with the ages and had been eclipsed by the advent of the *talkies*, or movies with a synchronized soundtrack. Brown (1930/2015) determined that the written word would advance only through innovation. The written word needed an equivalent of the talkies. It needed the "readies" (Bartram, 2014).

Brown (1930/2015) designed, but did not build, a reading machine through which a ribbon of miniaturized text would scroll behind a magnifying glass at a speed controlled by the reader and powered by an electric light plug (Schuessler, 2010). Brown (1930/2015) details the design in his book *The Readies*. Although the original distribution was limited to 150 copies, the book re-emerged in 2015 and is available in both "bottled up" (that is, print) and digital formats.

Fifteen years later, Ángela Ruiz Robles, an innovative teacher turned inventor, watched her students as they carried textbooks to and from school. Thinking about how her students might more easily access and carry multiple books, Robles designed an automated, if not digital, reader. Texts were printed onto spools stored in a portable device—one that easily fit into a 1940s-era schoolbag. Powered by compressed air, Robles's mechanical encyclopedia remains on display at the National Museum of Science and Technology in La Coruna, Spain (History-Computer.com, n.d.).

Our modern ebook may have been born in 1971 when University of Illinois student Michael Hart was exploring the Xerox Sigma 9 mainframe computer in the university's materials research department and wondered if access to the Advanced Research Projects Agency Network (ARPANET; the precursor to the internet) might be useful for purposes beyond data processing. Hart entered the text from a copy of the Declaration of Independence—one he picked up as part of a Fourth of July grocery store promotion—and sent it in a message via ARPANET (Project Gutenberg, n.d.). Six people downloaded the text. The first digital text had arrived. Later that year, Hart founded Project Gutenberg, the world's first internet library. At that point, digital was decided. We would add a new form of text to our world, and this new form of text expands its footprint daily.

It is apparent that digital is decided and will prevail in our business institutions and schools. Purchasing hardware, licensing software, upgrading networks, apps and bots, and artificial intelligence–infused innovations are all here to stay. A common refrain in the virtual age is to buy the latest and greatest device to stay relevant in a field that changes as swiftly as a streak of lightning. Yes, virtual learning is the place to be if we want to prepare students for the future.

What is yet to be decided are the full ramifications of digital media. Reading silently fundamentally altered the world of Ambrose and Augustine. Gutenberg's invention made text available to the masses. How will the advent of digital texts alter our perception of literacy? We need to explore how digital is different from previous forms of text.

Digital Is Different

At its core, reading is a complex cognitive process that involves decoding symbols to create meaning. From cave drawings to instant messaging, we are driven to leave a record of our experiences and just as driven to understand the experiences recorded by others. We create meaning from ancient cave art and rock carvings as we connect the images to our existing experiences (Grabianowski, 2008). The evidence suggests that thousands of years later, this cognitive process of associating meaning with images operates in much the same way. What we seek to understand is to what degree reading from digital, rather than printed, text impacts this cognitive process. In seeking this understanding, it makes sense to begin at the core of reading, which is decoding images, and work our way out to the potentially rough edges of sustained engagement and meaning creation.

Based on understandings gained via functional MRI technology, the core of reading—decoding images to create meaning—appears to remain constant. This cognitive process activates as we read both print and digital texts. Willingham (2017) explains that the mechanics of reading do not change when we move from digital to print and vice versa; however, our reading habits change to accommodate differences between print and digital. The distinction between digital and print becomes environmental. We operate in both print and digital environments; further, we adapt to the differences within each environment (Wolf, 2018). In the following sections, we'll explore how our reading habits differ in these print and digital environments, as well as how hyperlinks and other distractions come into play.

Reading Habits With Printed Text

When we learn to read, we master both the cognitive and physical processes of reading. As we discussed in chapter 1 (page 23), the cognitive process requires more than creating meaning from images; it requires associating sounds with letters, letter pairs, and high-frequency words to establish them in the brain's visual word form area (VWFA). When we encounter unknown or nonsense words, our brains elicit responses from a much wider pool of neurons in an effort to create meaning (Glezer, Kim, Rule, Jiang, & Riesenhuber, 2015).

In addition to the cognitive process, reading print involves some degree of physicality. The earliest reading was tactile—rubbing hands over images and tracing symbols carved in rocks. Likewise, printed books, newspapers, and magazines are tactile, three-dimensional, manipulatable objects. The tactile nature of reading printed texts can leave an impression, a physical memory. We tend to remember where within the text we read a specific quote, studied a graph, or were intrigued by an illustration—for example, toward the front, on the left-hand page, or close to the bottom (Willingham, 2017).

In learning to read, we also master *print awareness*, or the physical mechanics of reading, required to manipulate traditional text. We learn how a book works, reading left to right and from the top of the page to the bottom. We learn that books have covers and are filled with pages. We learn the vocabulary associated with reading: authors write books and illustrators create images, tables of contents help us navigate the text, and fly pages rarely include words. We learn to distinguish numbers from letters, uppercase from lowercase, and question marks from commas. Most of this comes through observation as loved ones model print awareness by reading aloud. All this learning merges the cognitive process of reading (phonological and phonemic awareness) with the physical process of reading (*concepts of print*, that is how to manipulate books and pages), mastering phonological, phonemic, and print awareness.

When engaged in print, readers typically set aside time for reading; with some, reading becomes part of their daily routine. Likewise, primarily print readers often establish a specific space for reading where the books are (such as a reading nook) while those who read digitally have continual access to books; the books go where they are. Also, the type of book that one reads may differ according to the physical space, for example, a novel in the reading nook, nonfiction in bed, and career-related material at the office. While reading from print, many readers tend to spend greater time with text and engage more in deep reading, rereading, annotating, and talking about what they read (Ackerman & Goldsmith, 2011). In further engagements with print, we physically add and remove sticky notes to mark key passages in the text. We add, but cannot remove, highlights. We write in the margin, and we ask the author to sign the title page.

Reading print creates a cognitive, tactile connection between reader and text. Reading print tends to be a specific, focused, purposeful, recursive, social endeavor, essentially a conversation between the reader and the author (Grice, 1975, as cited in Tierney, Anders, & Mitchell, 1987). The reader is engaged with one text at a time with no internal way to explore further, while reading digitally can offer access and engagement with multiple texts. The reader, in fact, is an essential part of the equation: "The existence of the text is a silent existence, silent until the moment in which a reader reads it. . . . All writing depends on the generosity of the reader" (Manguel, 1997, p. 276).

> *"The existence of the text is a silent existence, silent until the moment in which a reader reads it. . . . All writing depends on the generosity of the reader"* *(Manguel, 1997, p. 276).*

Reading Habits With Digital Text

There is something organic about print; we are physical beings continually engaging in a physical, paper-rich environment. At the same time, there is something innovative about reading digital texts, and we are as innovative as we are tactile. Studies suggest that many digital readers scan for keywords (word spotting) and read more selectively, rather than engaging in deep reading with sustained attention (Liu, 2005;

Sage, Augustine, Shand, Bakner, & Rayne, 2019). Word spotting is a noteworthy, creative habit (see figure 4.1).

Word spotting is a fast look at a text to spot key words that either explain something or give a synonym that further clarifies the meaning of the text. A quick glance over a section of the text often provides the cues and clues that help the reader make meaning of the text. This technique drives readers to go faster but generally with less depth of understanding than when reading in print. While it is true that screens are compelling for viewers young and old, readers still need some explicit instruction about reading effectively on digital devices.

Figure 4.1: Word spotting.

We do not just read from left to right. Rather, we read in a Z pattern—horizontal from left to right, diagonal down, and again left to right, corner to corner, on the next horizontal line (Witten, 2018; see figure 4.2).

In terms of digital reading choices, we can access news, entertainment, and information in the palm of our hand via our ever-present devices that respond to our needs. We have access to digital text to read whenever we have a moment. We no longer have to go where the books live; the digital versions travel with us.

For most of history, an increase in the quantity of reading has typically led to more learning. But the digital revolution has created a reading paradox, as we now spend more time reading (or perhaps viewing our handheld screen) but, in a general sense, we have not realized additional comprehension gains (Korbey, 2018). Part of this is intuitive. We instinctively suspect that while text messages and social media posts have proliferated, these forms of reading and writing have not aided literacy acquisition. But even when we read the digital versions of substantive writing, some differences in literacy acquisition may manifest. This typically occurs with longer texts.

Reading digitally is different—for some readers and with some texts. For most of us, reading a novel digitally is not so different from reading the same novel in print.

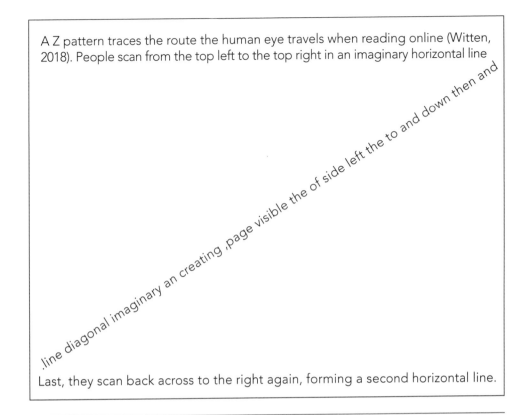

A Z pattern traces the route the human eye travels when reading online (Witten, 2018). People scan from the top left to the top right in an imaginary horizontal line and then and down to and the to left side of the page, visible creating an imaginary diagonal line. Last, they scan back across to the right again, forming a second horizontal line.

Figure 4.2: Z pattern example.

Following a recipe from a website is not so different from following a recipe from a cookbook. The digital difference becomes apparent when we read beyond pleasure and focus on information. When we read among multiple resources to understand and apply concepts, digital becomes distinctively different as we skim and scan the text (Liu, 2005; see figure 4.3, page 140).

Let's explore how and why habits change for us with certain texts and how we can overcome any differences. We tend to automatically do a lot of skimming, scanning, and scrolling for digital texts, yet we sometimes follow an F pattern for certain types of digital screen reading (Witten, 2018; see figure 4.4, page 140, for an example).

Distractions and the Brain's Modes of Operation

The potential for distraction is digital's constant companion (and the nemesis of focus and comprehension). One of the greatest of these is *hyperlinks*, or text that leads to a different location or page, which digital texts often contain. While a hyperlink may lead to useful information, it might also lead to something the reader already knows. At the very least, each embedded link is a decision. Do you click it or not?

In a 2005 study, Ziming Liu of San Jose State University found that when we read digitally, we do more scanning

and jumping around looking for keywords to get as much information as possible in a short amount of time.

In certain ways, digital reading is a less immersive experience than reading printed words.

Scanning text is a nonlinear form of reading, and when doing linear reading, without any skipping or jumping, we're engaged in deep reading. Deep reading allows for more immersion. In fact, nonlinear reading may influence comprehension. It's the difference between taking in the landscape from the window of a speeding car and taking a slow walk along the same route.

Figure 4.3: Skimming and scanning.

The F-shaped scanning pattern is characterized by many fixations concentrated at the top and the left side of the page.

Finally, users scan the content's left side vertically. This is normally a slow and systematic scan. Other times, users move faster. This last element forms the F's stem (Witten, 2018).

Users first read in a horizontal movement, usually across the upper part of the content area. This initial element forms the F's top bar.

Users next move down the page a bit and then read across in a second, shorter horizontal movement, forming the F's lower bar.

Figure 4.4: F pattern example.

Willingham (2017) notes that when reading online, the very presence of a hyperlink incurs a cognitive cost even if the reader chooses not to click the link.

Other studies suggest that many digital readers scan for keywords (word spotting) and read more selectively, rather than engaging in deep reading with sustained attention (Liu, 2005; Sage et al., 2019).

When we read digitally, we read more but spend less time with each individual text. We can fall into the trap of bouncing from text to text, following link after link until we have no idea where we are or how to go back to where we started. For some readers of digital texts, the evidence suggests a tendency toward reading the text one time rather than deep reading (Korbey, 2018; Liu, 2005).

It is logical that reading without fully attending to the text would manifest itself as an equal lack of deep thinking about the text. Amit Sood (2013), a doctor with the Mayo Clinic College of Medicine, writes that our brains operate in both focused and default modes. One is not better than the other; both are required for well-being. Sood (2013) points out that reading printed or digital texts, however, requires the focused mode, activating a "task-positive network" (p. 3), which effectively mutes other processes in order to fully immerse in the present task. We are fully immersed in the reading; our attention is focused inward. As Sood (2013) notes, various things are happening when you are in the focused state:

> As you read . . . your visual network is helping you see, your auditory network is keeping you aware of surrounding sounds, and your motor network is helping you sit upright. You also have a network that produces an ongoing dialogue in your head. To focus on reading, you have to mute that dialogue. (p. 2)

While the brain seems as if it is idling and relaxing a bit in the default mode, it is indeed much more active in this state (Sood, 2013). It is alert and attentive to every distraction. As we are spending an increasing amount of time reading electronic documents, a sense of screen-based reading behavior is emerging, and some of what we are coming to understand may be related to the brain's default mode. Perhaps digital readers operate more in the default mode, aware of distractions and failing to mute what Sood (2013) calls the *ongoing dialogue*. This screen-based reading behavior is, for many readers, characterized by more time spent browsing and scanning, keyword spotting, one-time reading, nonlinear reading, and selective reading, and less time spent in-depth reading and concentrated reading.

However, some readers may have yet to fully apply the focused mode when engaged with digital texts, even when response tools such as definitions and read-aloud functions are embedded in the digital platform. These may still be things we teachers must come to fully understand and then thoughtfully convey to our students when it comes to successfully negotiating different forms of reading—both print and digital. In the following section, we focus on the teacher's role in guiding all learners to become equally fluent, deliberate, and engaged in digital reading environments.

Digital Is Demanding

Reading a printed text requires a reader and some text gathered into a book, newspaper, magazine, brochure, flyer, billboard, or other medium. Reading a text digitally requires a reader, a device (charged or connected to a power source), text that has been coded and then gathered onto a digital platform or website, and internet connectivity to access or download the text. Indeed, digital is demanding. In fact, digital reading demands more because it is often an isolating experience because users are often focused so intently on the device with little attention to surroundings, and perhaps even less opportunity for conversation with other people. Rather than getting lost in a book, digital readers are perhaps lost in a device.

It's quite difficult to create and receive speech in an isolated environment. As mentioned earlier, reading is a social enterprise, a conversation between the reader and the author (Grice, 1975, as cited in Tierney et al., 1987). Therefore, in order to help students understand how to comprehend digital texts, we must build in multiple opportunities for them to think about what they are reading, to literally have a conversation with themselves, even pausing to annotate so they might share their thinking with others—in both spoken and written forms. As we've established, reading is born of listening and speaking; therefore, the phrase *reading is a conversation* is not just a metaphor but a scientific finding (National Aphasia Association, n.d.a; Romeo et al., 2018).

> *Reading is born of listening and speaking; therefore, the phrase* reading is a conversation *is not just a metaphor but a scientific finding (National Aphasia Association, n.d.a; Romeo et al., 2018).*

Reading demands conversation with ourselves when our own beliefs conflict with the claims made in the reading, or with others in imagined blog posts or unsent tweets—the ongoing back-and-forth that happens when ideas collide inside us and we can't let go. Even classroom conversations must be two-way streets. Otherwise, there's no outlet; the conversation is a dead end or a one-way broadcast from the front of the room, and it's frequently a "discussion," not a true back-and-forth dialogue.

In more structured classroom conversations, prior to reading, teachers begin with stating the purpose for reading, identifying a clear learning target, and giving expectations for success. Additionally, teachers anticipate knowledge and vocabulary gaps and design conversations to close those gaps. As illustrated in Schmoker's (2018) curriculum maps (see chapter 3, page 87), teachers must explicitly design conversations before reading occurs or when they are developing questions for close reading, for small-group discussion, and for writing about the reading.

When reading print, we annotate in the margins (or on sticky notes). Likewise, many ebook platforms allow the reader to annotate digital text, which seems to be a critical element for engagement. It lets readers converse with the author and with their own thinking. Many digital e-reader platforms also allow for shared conversations about the reading by including digital annotation tools. There are also online tools, such as Hypothesis (http://web.hypothes.is) and Diigo (www.diigo.com) that allow readers to engage in web-based conversations about what they read in digital books and websites. In the classroom, digital platforms such as myON Reader (www.myon.com) offer annotation and journaling tools for students. Teachers can create projects that encourage students to share their annotations and journal entries about their reading in ways that are meaningful to their learning. This paradigm shift allows multiple participants to connect, interact, and exchange ideas through the compelling experience of reading and conversing while anchored in the text. Figure 4.5 provides an example of digital annotation that is also a conversation.

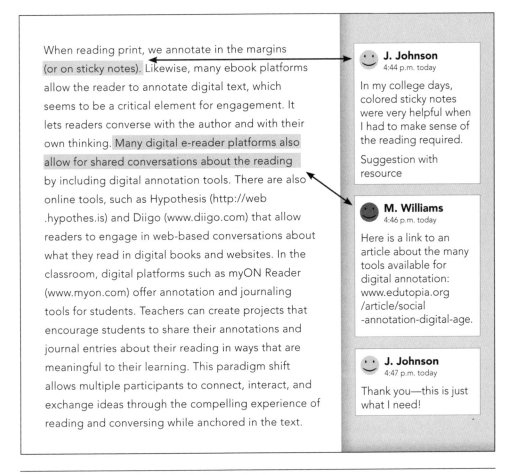

Figure 4.5: Example of digital annotation.

Blending digital reading with physical responses (for example, discussion and writing) may, in fact, negate some of the habits associated with distraction, scanning, and browsing rather than deep reading. Extending the reading conversation between the teacher and the student to peers can open the door to greater engagement in the text. Cooperative learning strategies require readers to return to the text for a deeper conversation. Learners casually discuss what they read with little, if any, guidance; however, rereading for academic purposes in the digital environment requires explicit instruction and modeling. For that, we return to the mechanics involved in reading, including the physical manipulation of digital text.

Of course, moving from print to digital is not the first adaptation in human reading history. This chapter opens with a history of print, from the advent of paper to the onset of digital texts. The Norwegian Broadcasting Corporation (NRK, 2007) offers an entertaining look at mastering print awareness as an adult, and with a new technology, in a skit called "Medieval Help Desk." In the skit, the reader moves from scroll technology to book technology, and we witness his struggle with print awareness. He succeeds with explicit instruction and modeling.

Students learning to thrive in the digital environment require just this sort of explicit instruction and modeling with digital texts. But, make no mistake about it, most need guidance for a fully developed sense of *digital awareness*, which is far more than learning to navigate a text. We suggest that digital awareness focus on four key elements: (1) perception, (2) purpose, (3) product, and (4) pace. We'll discuss each further in the following sections and in the Classroom Applications for this chapter.

Perception

Digital awareness means that students must recognize their perceptions of how they manage digital and print texts. The available evidence regarding students' perceptions of their learning from digital texts suggests a fascinating dichotomy. Studies include findings where students perceive they do better with printed texts, although the students have equally strong outcomes with print and digital. In contrast, students who perceive their outcomes are stronger when they use digital texts most often achieve more positive outcomes when reading print (Ackerman & Goldsmith, 2011; Mangen, Walgermo, & Bronnick, 2013; Singer & Alexander, 2017; Sullivan & Puntambekar, 2015).

Multiple studies focus on scrolling to navigate digital texts—in particular, how it taxes working memory and therefore holds the potential to negatively impact comprehension. For example, researchers Lauren M. Singer and Patricia A. Alexander (2017) write that the length of text (more than five hundred words) increases cognitive demand on the reader because of frequent scrolling and eye strain due to font size and backlighting, luminance, and contrast. They suggest that device characteristics may impact comprehension. Likewise, Christopher A. Sanchez and Jennifer Wiley (2009) share concerns about the negative association between scrolling and comprehension. But Sarah A. Sullivan and Sadhana Puntambekar (2015) find no significant difference in comprehension based on the demands of navigation (that is, scrolling). Comprehension differences noted when reading digital or printed texts for academic purposes appear to be more strongly connected to word count and goal-directed reading rather than to the print or digital environment (Sullivan & Puntambekar, 2015). Regardless, digital awareness includes students' acknowledgment and management of their perceptions of competence when working with digital or printed texts. Likewise, students should be aware of their state of mind prior to reading digital or printed texts lest a misperception of ability, based on format (digital or print), becomes a self-fulfilling prophecy.

We should nurture students' transition from the brain's default mode to its focused mode. We should also call on students to mute the dialogue of their environments to fully attend to reading physical books; this is as important with digital texts. For this, we will next explore the power of goal-directed, or purpose-driven, reading.

Purpose

Students need to understand the purpose for digital academic reading. What is the learning target, and why is the target best addressed with digital rather than printed texts? If, for example, the purpose for reading is to memorize Lincoln's Gettysburg Address (UShistory.org, n.d.), students may have little need for anything beyond a printed copy. If, however, the purpose for reading is to analyze Lincoln's word choice and rationale for referencing the Declaration of Independence rather than the U.S. Constitution in the address, they may require access to multiple texts related to the address.

The concept of using technology to coordinate multiple texts is not new. The 16th century Italian engineer Agostino Ramelli designed the bookwheel, a device that would give readers access to multiple texts in a single platform ("Agostino Ramelli," n.d.). As a result of continued innovation, teachers must address the potential for distraction, and students must begin learning with a manageable number of resources, each vetted for accuracy and direct connection to the purpose as they develop evidence, or the product, of their learning.

Product

In chapter 3 (page 87), you looked at two curriculum documents (figures 3.3 and 3.4, pages 110–112) and likely noted that some reading tasks include a tangible *product* (anything students produce; for example, a writing assignment) while other tasks focus more on observable products or processes (for example, discussion, note taking, or questioning). For student-created products, teachers should lead the way with purpose, explicit instruction, and modeling. Students benefit when they see examples of acceptable and outstanding work as well as work that falls short of the task.

According to assessment experts Paul Black and Dylan Wiliam (1998), low achievement is often the result of students' unawareness of expectations. Just as digital reading for academic purposes must be purpose driven, so, too, must students' products of learning reflect deliberate, focused effort. For that, we look at the pace of reading digitally.

Pace

Many readers likely recognize *citius, altius, fortius* as the Olympic motto, which means "faster, higher, stronger" (International Olympic Committee, n.d.). This motto has inspired thousands of athletes. But how could it inspire readers?

A key component of digital awareness focuses on the pace of reading; pace goes beyond speed. Just as an Olympic marathoner who can pace him- or herself in a deliberate way may seem to start out slow but can still win the race, a reader must also value pace over speed, especially when working with digital text. To create a reading motto based on the Olympic motto, we should change *citius* (or "faster") to *tardius* (or "slower"), as our goal with reading must be to slow down. Students typically read faster with digital text than with printed text; unsurprisingly, students who read faster retain less of what they read. This is complicated by the fact that students who read fast think they are actually doing much better because they equate speed with competence (Singer & Alexander, 2017). Because students are unlikely to slow themselves down, it's up to teachers to consider pace in the context of students' perception of their digital reading speed, their purpose for reading, and (when appropriate) the kind of evidence they create to demonstrate mastery.

Further, pace should consider the length of text. We are learning that there is little, if any, significant difference in comprehension when students work with digital texts that are five to eight hundred words long (Singer & Alexander, 2017). Teachers should let students in on this finding and follow through with opportunities for them to practice reading, and rereading, with brief digital texts. They should design lessons with opportunities for *deeper* reading of shorter passages followed by conversation. This is not to say that teachers should use only short passages for academic purposes; however, breaking longer texts into more manageable segments may support stronger learning outcomes (Singer & Alexander, 2017). In the Olympic motto, *altius* means "higher." Interestingly, *altius* is also the Latin word for "deeper." Likewise, we often use *higher* and *deeper* interchangeably when referring to comprehension ability (for example, *higher levels of comprehension* is equivalent to *deeper levels of comprehension*).

Finally, pace focuses on patience, which in our Olympic metaphor equates to *fortius*—"stronger." Keeping the brain focused on a text requires the strength of mind to be patient. Teachers should guide students to exercise their patience with reading digital texts in order to overcome their impatience with boredom. Abundant access to digital technologies has not resulted in the inability to sustain attention; rather, it has increased our "impatience with boredom" (Willingham, 2017, p. 173). We have everything at our fingertips, yet we are bored. We think we have little cognitive patience for deep reading on a device designed for the moment; however, to circle back to the first of our elements of digital awareness, it is our *perception* of what is worthy of our attention that promotes deep reading, rather than the format in which we access a text (Willingham, 2017).

When reading for academic purposes, *stronger* comprehension gains are often the result of having engaged more deeply in shorter texts read more slowly and deliberately. In keeping with our Olympic metaphor, when it comes to digital reading, slow the pace and engage in deeper reading with strong patience to achieve better outcomes—*tardius, altius, fortius.*

> *It is our perception of what is worthy of our attention that promotes deep reading, rather than the format in which we access a text (Willingham, 2017).*

We began this section with the statement that digital is demanding. Digital demands conversation, awareness, and a focused mind. Digital demands that we acknowledge our perceptions, engage in purposeful reading, demonstrate evidence of competence when reading for academic purposes, and attend to the length of a text and our pace in reading it. In the following section, we continue our focus on reading for academic purposes as we explore ways that exceptional teaching and access to meaningful digital and print texts can combine to bring about dynamic outcomes.

Classroom Applications for Teachers

For this chapter on digital reading, we begin our classroom applications with children who haven't yet entered a classroom because we want to address the relationship of early learning and digital reading. The issue of screen time for very young children is a controversial one. But we believe that technology has a place in a dynamic learning environment for young children even before they begin their years of schooling. Once we've discussed some examples for these children, we'll move on to explore how this foundation leads into digital reading throughout students' school years. Rather than list specific strategies for a field as vast and fluid as digital literacy, for this chapter we have chosen to focus in a more general sense on how teachers can approach it as students progress through school.

Digital Reading and Young Children (Toddlers to PreK)

How does digital media affect young children in the preliteracy stage? Research published in the *Journal of the American Medical Association Pediatrics* (see Hutton,

Dudley, Horowitz-Kraus, DeWitt, & Holland, 2019) details a study of digital media consumption among forty-seven children between the ages of three and five who were not yet independent readers. Over the course of fifteen months, researchers sought to understand if the amount of screen-based media time impacts ongoing development in the parts of the brain associated with language and literacy. While the researchers acknowledge limitations of the study, their findings are meaningful in discussions about learning to read.

Twenty-eight children who participated in the study (60 percent) had their own portable devices; the remaining nineteen participants (40 percent) had *access* to portable devices or televisions in their bedrooms. The children's median screen time, as reported by their parents, averaged 1.5 hours per day. The researchers state that, although findings show a negative correlation between screen-based media consumption and brain development, establishing causation (that is, showing that 1.5 hours of screen-based media time per day negatively impact brain development) is beyond the scope of the study (Hutton et al., 2019). However, they write that the critical factor to examine concerns the potential that "human interactive (e.g., shared reading) time" is *displaced* by screen-based media (Hutton et al., 2019, p. 6).

Reading, as the researchers note, is a uniquely human and complex social enterprise that requires uniquely human interaction (see also Bryan, 2018). In early learning, the most powerful dynamic of reading from digital and print books is perhaps found in social interaction between children and caring adults. Adults' *perceptions* of literacy development in young children—in particular, their perception of the power of human interaction in learning to read—are critical. Within this human interaction, we find both the *purpose* and the *product* of reading digital and print texts aloud to young children. As discussed earlier (see Read-Alouds in the Classroom in chapter 1, page 36), reading aloud to students builds vocabulary, develops listening comprehension, deepens knowledge, and strengthens emotional bonds (Lemov et al., 2016; Trelease, 2013; Willingham, 2017). This power is available when parents read aloud to their children from print and digital texts.

As an example, we may look at many young learners' favorite book, *Chicka Chicka Boom Boom*, written by Bill Martin Jr. and John Archambault (1989) and illustrated by Lois Ehlert. The delightful rhythm and rhyme scheme demand a read-aloud:

> A told B,
> And B told C,
> "I'll meet you at the top
> of the coconut tree." (p. 1)

In 1995, to the delight of many, a CD-ROM version of *Chicka Chicka Boom Boom* was released (Martin & Archambault, 1995). This led to millions of children being able to chant, "Chicka chicka boom boom," along with Ray Charles's narration on the recording. They were able to hear an interpretation of the words that was different from their parents or caregivers. Less than a decade later, *Chicka Chicka Boom Boom* was released as an ebook. The technological evolution of *Chicka Chicka Boom Boom* made the text more accessible; however, young children perceive the book to be worthy of their attention not because of that but because of the delight they find in sharing the text with adults.

Eric Carle's (2013) *Animal Babies* offers an ideal blend of embedded technology and printed book, especially for a book meant to be read aloud. By design, this is a lap read (that is, the child sits on the parent's lap while the parent reads the book aloud). It provides an ideal setting to guide young children through the joy to be found in rhythm, rhyme, repetition, images, and sounds—each of which is an important aspect of phonological awareness. For example, the following passage captures the joy to be found in this book's writing:

> The fox and his kit play and run.
> The seal and her pup sit in the sun.
> The penguin keeps his chick safe and warm.
> The bear guides her cub out of the storm. (Carle, 2013, pp. 1–8)

The book includes a plastic tab that features buttons for each animal featured. With each page, toddlers have access to the tab so they can press the animal's corresponding button (for example, the image of the seal pup or the fox kit) and hear the sound the animal makes. Toddlers quickly learn to do this with little direct instruction and modeling from adults. As stated previously, the brain first sees letters and words as images and seeks to create meaning for the images by associating them with sounds. As toddlers squeal with laughter and imitate the baby animal sounds, their brains are quite busy building these correspondences based on the adult's read-aloud and the animal sounds. This shows how a digitally enhanced text can further enhance the child's interaction with a caring adult.

In the following section, we explore how that interaction expands when school comes into play.

Digital Reading in Grades PreK–3

The body of evidence regarding digital texts and their potential impact on young learners is still emerging; however, a 2017 study of preschoolers' developing word-recognition skills has yielded intriguing insights that may impact our perception of reading digitally at these grades (Zipke, 2017). Elementary and special education professor Marcy Zipke (2017) conducted two experiments to explore the impact of reading digital storybooks on a tablet. In the first experiment, twenty-five preschoolers, ages four to five (all emergent readers in a school setting), explored a story from a digital storybook using the read-aloud function on their tablets (their *purpose*). Their word-recognition scores (their *products*) were significantly higher when they engaged with the digital storybook using the read-aloud function than when the same story in a printed book was read aloud to them by their teacher. However, comprehension scores were not significantly different between the digital storybook and the comparable printed book.

In the second experiment, these same students had access to two additional stories in the digital storybook. They explored the first book at their own *pace* using the read-aloud function, this time with additional animations embedded in the digital storybook made available. During their engagement with the second digital book, the teacher implemented a guided talk about the text, which may have impacted pace. Surprisingly, both word-recognition scores *and* comprehension scores were higher when students explored on their own than when the teacher guided talk about the story. Zipke (2017) posits multimedia (such as highlighting and word tracking) may have impacted higher word-recognition scores.

Zipke (2017) also references use of embedded tools available on these platforms in her commentary from the first experiment. However, after both experiments, she concludes, with emphasis, that digital storybooks are *not* a substitute for adult interaction. While children showed they could perform well independently, we should not consider allowing children to interact only with digital texts. In fact, adult interaction is critical, but with the right degree of age-appropriate and purpose-driven engagement, these students learn remarkably well on their own.

Perceptions about reading digital and printed text in the primary grades also focus on developmentally appropriate engagements with text. Again, the purpose for reading is found in developing vocabulary, building background knowledge, and gradually becoming independent readers. From the Zipke (2017) study, we find that the products of reading—in this case, solely reading digital texts—are recognizing words, growing in comprehension, and finding joy in reading. However, an additional product of reading in both print and digital texts is the development of *prosody* (reading with expressiveness, intonation, rhythm, and emphasis to certain words). Prosodic reading, like decoding, is a gradually developed skill, best taught via extensive modeling. With digital texts incorporating narration (often by professional actors) and text tracking via highlights, developing prosody becomes a concomitant product of reading digitally.

In addition, primary students engage in vast amounts of writing. Occasionally responding in writing to digital and printed texts is (or certainly should be) a natural experience for them. Written responses at this age group might include writing down two things they learned from reading informational text or drawing a character or event from the text and explaining it to others. Pace is foundational in each student's reading development; therefore, finding appropriate texts (in both readability and interest) becomes a hallmark of these grades. In this case, pace also impacts the product. For these students, appropriate writing tasks work well with digital text.

Digital Reading in Grades 4–6

In the intermediate grades, most readers have gained control of the mechanics of reading and read for distinct purposes (for example, to learn, to practice, to complete a task, to escape in an adventure, or to laugh). With explicit instruction and modeling, intermediate students learn to apply their developing sense of digital awareness to set an appropriate pace for reading digitally and, especially while they are reading online, to control distractions. Self-regulation is required.

Again, we turn to traditional strategies to help intermediate students learn to self-regulate when reading digitally. It begins with pace. Digital reading expert Devin Hess believes the first priority is to slow readers down so they focus on the text rather than the distractions (as cited in Schwartz, 2016). To build the capacity for distraction-free reading, we should begin with brief passages. We should let students know that the purpose for reading is twofold: (1) to learn from the content and (2) to regulate their ability to focus on the text and ignore (mute) distractions. By identifying the purpose for reading and giving students a technique to mute distractions, we guide them toward positive perceptions of themselves as competent print and digital readers. Finally, we must establish a product following the reading for students to demonstrate comprehension. Again, we turn to writing.

Intermediate students, like primary and high school students, benefit from writing as a reflection. Hess advocates engaging students in a *four-word headline strategy* (as cited in Schwartz, 2016). After a review of authentic headlines from other sources, intermediate students summarize a brief piece of digital reading with four words. Each student's four-word headline should reflect the key ideas in the reading. Then students gather in groups of four to compare and defend their word choices. This can take place either in turns in front of the whole class, or the teacher can circulate around the room while all groups interact at the same time. The teacher should be checking for understanding as students defend their word choices.

Digital Reading in Grades 7–8

In a study of 109 middle school students, literacy professor and researcher Julie Coiro (2011) finds a positive correlation between prior knowledge and reading online for academic purposes. Further, she finds that for students with low levels of reading comprehension skills, their degree of background knowledge has a significant positive effect on comprehension while reading online. This echoes the discussion in chapter 3 (page 87) and is also connected to students' perceptions of how well they read online. Teachers must take care that students' perception of reading well online matures to a strong sense of self-regulation, which is essential to actually reading well online. Again, effective instructional strategies apply.

To establish purpose for reading, teachers can turn to an adaptation of the familiar KWL strategy (see Bryan, 1998, and the activity on page 121), where a teacher challenges students' thinking to generate interest in what may seem like a settled topic (for example, Lincoln's Gettysburg Address; UShistory.org, n.d.). Students identify what they think they know about the famous speech. Rather than asking what they want to learn about the address, the teacher leads students into a discussion of myths and misconceptions, or what we still need to know about the address. Once they have generated some questions, the teacher demonstrates self-regulation in searching for online resources, modeling how to trust sites and vet for bias. In this case, there is a wealth of information at the Library of Congress (www.loc.gov) and other trusted sites, such as the History Channel (www.history.com), the National Museum of American History (https://americanhistory.si.edu, the Smithsonian Institution Archives (https://siarchives.si.edu/collections), and the Google News Archive (https://news .google.com/newspapers). Students, via instruction and modeling, understand that self-regulation while working and reading online is as important as while reading a digital book.

The teacher forms students into teams. Then the teacher visits with each team, again focusing on self-regulation, as the teams begin their work. Students first determine their product; will they do an oral report, a presentation, a written piece, or an online post? The product informs the online search for resources (for example, selecting a video for a potential oral or written product would make little sense because the focus would be developing literacy rather than relying on technology). Students also take an active role in their pace, as within their teams they acknowledge schedules but still find common times to meet to work on their project.

Digital Reading in Grades 9–12

A comparison of twelfth graders' reading habits from the 1970s through 2016 yields insights worthy of concern (Twenge, Martin, & Spitzberg, 2019). In the 1970s, 60 percent of twelfth graders reported that they read a book or magazine each day. By 2016, only 16 percent of twelfth graders were reading a book or magazine each day (Twenge et al., 2019; see figure 4.6). If today's high school students are not reading print or digital books or magazines, what, if anything, are they reading? Certainly, we can assume that access to digital media via smartphones has gone up considerably, and that has contributed to the drop in reading. These teens spend an average of nine hours per day with digital media, including games, with less than one hour on social media. Further, despite advanced digital devices, teens devote very little time to creating their own content (Common Sense Media, 2019).

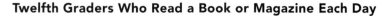

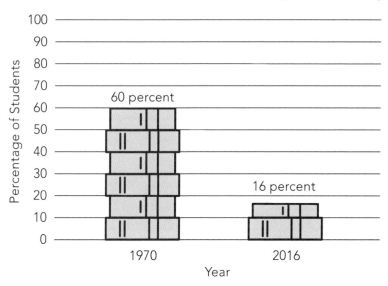

Twelfth Graders Who Read a Book or Magazine Each Day

Source: Twenge et al., 2019.

Figure 4.6: Twelfth graders' reading habits.

Students, who may be eager consumers of digital content, remain reluctant to engage deeply in reading digitally for academic purposes. It is in this context that we must explore how to achieve dynamic outcomes among learners who read little and write less. The following fictional scenario recounts an authentic example of a project that helps students truly engage in digital reading in a life-changing way.

Confronted with the prospect of a monthlong project on Africa, a disinterested student grumbles that she does not know how to create a PowerPoint and is never going to Africa. What good would this project do her in life? The teacher in this fictional, authentic example is able to tell her, having planned out this project carefully, that the *purpose* of the project is to encourage geographical interest in African countries, update *perceptions* about those countries, and master the skill of self-regulation over distractions while reading online. For this project, students consume and summarize online content. The teacher gives them autonomy in designing their *product* of learning, although it is subject to the teacher's approval to ensure it meets rubric requirements. The goal is for the final product to match each student's unique talents. The teacher sets expectations for originality, creativity, and accuracy. Further, the teacher establishes the concept of *pace* and self-regulation in using digital resources by requiring that students give an update each Friday throughout the four-week project. The scope of the project requires students to select three of Africa's fifty-four countries and plan a multiweek visit. In doing so, students engage in extensive online research to determine, for example, the immunizations required prior to travel, the process to obtain a passport, the overall climate and its impact on packing choices, and the location and contact information of the American embassy.

At the culmination of the project, students, including the one cited previously who could not imagine how this assignment would ever impact her life, offer insightful comments on their feedback forms. In particular, students write about their evolving perceptions of Africa, its history, its diversity, its size, and its multiple nations. Additionally, students reflect on their developing digital skills that continue to serve them.

The teacher reflects on the transition that her disinterested student made in the course of the project:

> Four weeks later, when I walked in the room, the first thing I saw was the suitcase, and I knew it was hers! She acknowledged her perception of her digital skills, demonstrated the advances she had made with those skills, and used her creativity to illustrate her increased interest in Africa. She filled that suitcase with maps, tickets, clothing, replicas of currency, photographs of historical and cultural sites, souvenirs, and access to a podcast with authentic translations of foreign phrases. It was extraordinary.
>
> Five years later, I was astounded to receive a postcard from her while she was in the Republic of Mali, in western Africa, where she was completing a humanitarian mission. I still wonder if she took that suitcase!

This dynamic outcome was realized through exceptional teaching and the student's willingness to reframe her perception of what she deemed was worthy of her attention.

This chapter on reading digitally began with Socrates railing against the introduction of paper to education and now concludes with a young woman overcoming discomfort with digital tools and traveling to the Republic of Mali via inspiration born of a high school social studies project. Digital text is here to stay, but paper is not going anywhere; adapting to and integrating both expand literacy and knowledge, as well as the horizons of everyone who uses these tools. To guide further investigation, we include collaborative team questions and additional resources for your exploration.

PLC Discussion Questions

We provide these discussion questions for use within department or grade-level teams. If your school functions as a professional learning community, these questions are an effective way to encourage professional dialogue in your collaborative team. Conversations like this are key to building trust within the team and helping team members learn from one another. Choose one or several based on interest and concerns exposed during a book study or independent reading of this book.

- Working as a grade-level or campus team, share your thinking regarding Sood's (2013) work on the brain's focused and default modes. Have you noticed students transitioning from focused to default? If so, how have you guided them back toward focused? Which strategies either from this chapter or from your repertoire do you find effective?

- Which of the strategies listed in this chapter have you tried? What did you observe? How did you adapt the strategies to meet your instructional purposes?

- How do digital readers get derailed as they seek to engage in closer, deeper reading? What strategies might be most effective in keeping students on track?

- How would you analyze and adapt perception, purpose, product, and pace for leading students to greater digital awareness and deeper engagement with digital texts?

Resources for Learning More

Amit Sood's (2013) techniques (described at www.resilientoption.com) are a great resource to learn about focusing the brain.

Sarah D. Sparks's (2016) *Education Week* blog post "Screens vs. Print: Does Digital Reading Change How Students Get the Big Picture?" is a source of great practical advice for teachers.

To access the only known photo of Lincoln at Gettysburg, go to the Library of Congress website (www.loc.gov/pictures/item/2012648250). Go to https://prologue.blogs.archives.gov/2010/11/19/rare-photo-of-lincoln-at-gettysburg to see an enlargement of the photo of Lincoln at Gettysburg, in which Lincoln is more visible.

To access multiple resources on Africa or any continent or country, visit the Central Intelligence Agency's website (https://www.cia.gov/library/publications/the-world-factbook), which has a useful world fact book.

CONCLUSION
The Promise of Literacy Reframed

We started this book with a decidedly elegant French word, *repoussoir*. When we first encountered this word, our phonics failed us. We did not even know how to pronounce the word, blaming that on our bad French, not on our lack of phonics instruction. It was only when we spotted the prefix *re-*, meaning "again," that we had our first clue—doing something again or repeating it. That was when we started to get excited.

Repoussoir. Yes, this word put us on the right track. We liked it. It sounded just right. We had been searching for a word to describe the restructuring, redoing, and reappraising of our failing approach to reading; it had been right on the tip of our tongues. And there it was: *reframing* literacy. We needed desperately to help ourselves and others understand our mission to address troubling findings that reading growth continues to stall despite heroic efforts, massive funding, and documented evidence. Research has signaled it isn't working when any public school teacher could tell you it isn't. Our students can't read. Some can. But far too many can't. It's a hard truth that we must address. The time is now.

The Many Gifts of Literacy Reframed

Now, we have a beautiful, hope-filled word, *repoussoir*, fueling us as we go on ahead with our ideas about what teachers might do to dramatically shift their approach to literacy and lead to student reading success. And we proceeded to unleash the three learnings we had embraced to encourage reading success across our schools: (1) decoding, (2) vocabulary, and (3) knowledge. Decoding, vocabulary, and knowledge are, after all, the usual suspects of literacy learning, yet we knew we needed to give them a creative reboot so we would gain a new perspective on them—a repoussoir, if you will. And that is exactly what we have tried to do.

So now we direct our view to our completed book, *Literacy Reframed*. We said at the beginning that our goal was to explore three well-established elements of literacy and reframe these familiar ideas to refocus our approach to literacy learning and capture findings we value. In fact, these seminal conversations offer the promise of favorable literacy journeys for all readers, regardless of their talents and needs. These ideas offer words to ponder and discuss that will help you define your literacy vision and collectively determine how you will proceed with your accepted mission: to equip your students as literate, caring citizens prepared for known and unknown challenges in the world they live in. These engaged citizens are the priceless gifts that literacy reframed promises.

One More Glimpse Into a Literacy Reframed Classroom

Let's take a moment to revisit the classroom scenes we envisioned to show how commonsense ideas can replace the obsession with skill work. As you reflect on the positive consequences of this long-overdue, game-changing shift, the most important impact you can expect is students' renewed joy in discovery as they become motivated by their natural curiosities and gnawing desire to find out more by reading. Rich content is the golden nugget that drives reading; the right balance of skills makes it possible to pan for the gold.

The Lyrical Sound of Literacy

The most noticeable difference in a literacy reframed classroom is the sound of sputtered reading, fluent reading, choral reading, and paired reading, reading voices chiming in all around the room. These students are consumed with reading—reading a book, reading a digital screen, reading in pairs in science, or just listening to the teacher reading aloud a difficult passage in mathematics, punctuated with comments of clarification. Other notable behaviors you hear in this knowledge-centered approach are student-to-student dialogues, discussions, debates, arguments, and compromises as students continually question each other's points of view. These are the sounds that heighten the senses of eager learners.

The Remarkable Look of Literacy

The hallmark of the look of reading is words, words, words. Yes, that's it in a nutshell. Vocabulary acquisition is an absolute when developing strong, fluent readers with a wide, broad, deep, and imaginative vocabulary that adds words to the mind faster than the blink of an eye. Readers find new words everywhere they look, in everything they read, from historical novels to historical biographies; from comic books to primary picture books; from grade-level science books to local news articles; and from words and images seen on classroom SMART Boards to the 24/7 flow of bytes that come across our e-readers and tablets.

The Kaleidoscopic Knowingness of Literacy

In a knowledge-centric classroom, targeted knowledge becomes the motivational spark to hook students on reading. Have students read a word, a sentence, a paragraph, or a chapter, and then have them stop and determine the text's takeaway. After all, knowledge-centric reading goes far beyond the mechanics of reading. It is about what we draw from reading—the knowingness, information, insight, or enlightenment it renders. That's the only test of knowledge we need—the knowingness that connects, expands, and punctuates our quest for learning. And once we have embarked on that quest, the only way to keep it going is to just read, every day and in every way.

References and Resources

Ackerman, R., & Goldsmith, M. (2011). Metacognitive regulation of text learning: On screen versus on paper. *Journal of Experimental Psychology: Applied, 17*(1), 18–32.

Agostino Ramelli. (n.d.). In *Wikipedia*. Accessed at https://en.wikipedia.org/wiki/Agostino _Ramelli on April 10, 2020.

Al-Darayseh, A.-M. A. (2014). The impact of using explicit/implicit vocabulary teaching strategies on improving students' vocabulary and reading comprehension. *Theory and Practice in Language Studies, 4*(6), 1109–1118.

American Library Association. (2019). *Digital literacy*. Accessed at https://literacy.ala.org/digital -literacy on March 5, 2020.

Anderson, R. C., Hiebert, E. H., Scott, J. A., & Wilkinson, I. A. G. (1985). *Becoming a nation of readers: The report of the Commission on Reading*. Washington, DC: National Academy of Education.

Anderson, R., & Nagy, W. (1993). *The vocabulary conundrum* (Technical Report No. 570). Urbana, IL: Center for the Study of Reading.

Arena, J. I. (Ed.). (1969). *Teaching through sensory-motor experiences*. Novato, CA: Academic Therapy Publications.

Aronson, E., & Patnoe, S. (2011). *Cooperation in the classroom: The jigsaw method*. London: Pinter & Martin.

Arya, D. J., Hiebert, E. H., & Pearson, P. D. (2011). The effects of syntactic and lexical complexity on the comprehension of elementary science texts. *International Electronic Journal of Elementary Education, 4*(1), 107–125.

Ashton-Warner, S. (1963). *Teacher*. New York: Touchstone.

Barrs, M., & Cork, V. (2001). *The reader in the writer: The links between the study of literature and writing development at key stage 2*. London: Centre for Language in Primary Education.

Bartram, M. (2014, March 10). *The history of ebooks from 1930's "readies" to today's GPO ebook services*. Accessed at https://govbooktalk.gpo.gov/2014/03/10/the-history-of-ebooks-from-1930s-readies-to-todays-gpo-ebook-services on March 6, 2020.

Beck, I. L., McKeown, M. G., & Kucan, L. (2013). *Bringing words to life: Robust vocabulary instruction* (2nd ed.). New York: Guilford Press.

Binder, J. R. (2015). The Wernicke area: Modern evidence and a reinterpretation. *Neurology, 85*(24), 2170–2175.

Black, P., & Wiliam, D. (1998). Inside the black box: Raising standards through classroom assessment. *Phi Delta Kappan, 80*(2), 139–148.

Bloom, B. S. (1956). *Taxonomy of educational objectives: The classification of educational goals*. New York: Longman.

Boroditsky, L. (2019). Language and the brain. *Science, 366*(6461), 13. Accessed at https://science.sciencemag.org/content/366/6461/13 on June 22, 2020.

Bowers, J. S. (2020). Reconsidering the evidence that systematic phonics is more effective than alternative methods of reading instruction. *Educational Psychology Review*. Accessed at https://link.springer.com/article/10.1007/s10648-019-09515-y on April 2, 2020.

Brown, B. (2015). *The readies* (C. Saper, Ed.). New York: Roving Eye Press. (Original work published 1930)

Brown, R. M. (1983). *Sudden death*. New York: Bantam Books.

Bryan, J. (1998). KWWL: Questioning the known. *The Reading Teacher, 51*(7), 618–620.

Bryan, J. (2018, January 11). *The teacher as reading coach: Relationship-building that motivates students to read and achieve their personalized goals* [Blog post]. Accessed at www.renaissance.com/2018/01/11/blog-teacher-reading-coach-relationship-building-motivates-students-read-achieve-personalized-goals on March 5, 2020.

Calhoun, E. F. (1999). *Teaching beginning reading and writing with the Picture Word Inductive Model*. Alexandria, VA: Association for Supervision and Curriculum Development.

Carle, E. (2013). *Animal babies*. Phoenix, AZ: Phoenix International.

Carnine, D. W, Silbert, J., Kame'enui, E. J., Slocum, T. A., & Travers, P. (2017). *Direct instruction reading* (6th ed.). Upper Saddle River, NJ: Pearson.

Carroll, L. (1871). *Jabberwocky* [Poem]. Accessed at www.poetryfoundation.org/poems/42916/jabberwocky on April 5, 2020.

Castles, A., Rastle, K., & Nation, K. (2018). Ending the reading wars: Reading acquisition from novice to expert. *Psychological Science in the Public Interest, 19*(1), 5–51.

Cervetti, G. N., Wright, T. S., & Hwang, H. (2016). Conceptual coherence, comprehension, and vocabulary acquisition: A knowledge effect? *Reading and Writing: An Interdisciplinary Journal, 29*(4), 761–779.

Coiro, J. (2011). Predicting reading comprehension on the internet: Contributions of offline reading skills, online reading skills, and prior knowledge. *Journal of Literacy Research, 43*(4), 352–392. Accessed at https://journals.sagepub.com/doi/pdf/10.1177/1086296X11421979 on March 6, 2020.

Common Sense Media. (2019). *The Common Sense census: Media use by tweens and teens, 2019.* Accessed at www.commonsensemedia.org/research/the-common-sense-census-media-use-by-tweens-and-teens-2019 on March 6, 2020.

Conley, D. T. (2005). *College knowledge: What it really takes for students to succeed and what we can do to get them ready.* San Francisco: Jossey-Bass.

Coyle, D. (2012). *The little book of talent: 52 tips for improving your skills.* New York: Bantam.

Crane, S. (1895). *The red badge of courage.* New York: Appleton & Company.

Cromley, J. G. (2009). Reading achievement and science proficiency: International comparisons from the Programme on International Student Assessment. *Reading Psychology, 30*(2), 89–118.

Dehaene, S. (2009). *Reading in the brain: The new science of how we read.* New York: Penguin.

Diamond, M. C., & Hopson, J. L. (1999). *Magic trees of the mind: How to nurture your child's intelligence, creativity, and healthy emotions from birth through adolescence.* New York: Penguin.

Dickens, C. (1973). *Great expectations.* Oxford, England: Oxford University Press. (Original work published 1861)

DuFour, R., DuFour, R., Eaker, R., & Karhanek, G. (2004). *Whatever it takes: How professional learning communities respond when kids don't learn.* Bloomington, IN: Solution Tree Press.

DuFour, R., DuFour, R., Eaker, R., Many, T. W., & Mattos, M. (2016). *Learning by doing: A handbook for Professional Learning Communities at Work* (3rd ed.). Bloomington, IN: Solution Tree Press.

Dweck, C. S. (2006). *Mindset: The new psychology of success.* New York: Random House.

Ede, L. (1987). New perspectives on the speaking-writing relationship: Implications for teachers of basic writing. In T. Enos (Ed.), *A sourcebook for basic writing teachers.* New York: Random House.

Education Endowment Foundation. (n.d.). *Phonics.* Accessed at https://educationendowmentfoundation.org.uk/evidence-summaries/teaching-learning-toolkit/phonics on April 11, 2020.

Elementary and Secondary Education Act of 1965, Pub. L. No. 89-10, § 79, Stat. 27 (1965).

Enokida, K. (2016). Digital story (re)telling using graded readers and smartphones. In S. Papadima-Sophocleous, L. Bradley, & S. Thouësny (Eds.), *CALL communities and culture: Short papers from EUROCALL 2016* (pp. 132–136). Dublin, Ireland: Research-Publishing.net.

Ericsson, A., & Pool, R. (2017). *Peak: Secrets from the new science of expertise.* New York: Random House.

Ferguson, M. (1980). *The Aquarian conspiracy: Personal and social transformation in the 1980s.* Los Angeles: Tarcher.

Fogarty, R. J. (2007). *Literacy matters: Strategies every teacher can use.* Thousand Oaks, CA: Corwin Press.

Fogarty, R. J., Kerns, G. M., & Pete, B. M. (2018). *Unlocking student talent: The new science of developing expertise.* New York: Teachers College Press.

Fox, M. (1984). *Wilfrid Gordon McDonald Partridge.* La Jolla, CA: Kane Miller.

Fox, M. (2008). *Reading magic: Why reading aloud to our children will change their lives forever.* Boston: Harcourt.

Frith, U. (1985). Beneath the surface of developmental dyslexia. In K. Patterson, J. C. Marshall, & M. Coltheart (Eds.), *Surface dyslexia: Neuropsychological and cognitive studies of phonological reading* (pp. 301–330). London: Routledge.

Fromme, A., Cutraro, J., & Schulten, K. (2012, December 5). *Lab lit: Writing fiction based on real science* [Blog post]. Accessed at https://learning.blogs.nytimes.com/2012/12/05/lab-lit -writing-fiction-based-on-real-science on March 6, 2020.

Garrison, S. (2016, September 23). *What are "text sets," and why use them in the classroom?* Accessed at https://fordhaminstitute.org/national/commentary/what-are-text-sets-and-why -use-them-classroom on March 6, 2020.

Giff, P. R. (1997). *Lily's crossing.* New York: Delacorte Press.

Gilkerson, J., Richards, J. A., Warren, S. F., Montgomery, J. K., Greenwood, C. R., Oller, D. K., et al. (2017). Mapping the early language environment using all-day recordings and automated analysis. *American Journal of Speech-Language Pathology, 26*(2), 248–265.

Glezer, L. S., Kim, J., Rule, J., Jiang, X., & Riesenhuber, M. (2015). Adding words to the brain's visual dictionary: Novel word learning selectively sharpens orthographic representations in the VWFA. *Journal of Neuroscience, 35*(12), 4965–4972.

Goodman, A. (2006). *Intuition.* New York: Dial Press.

Gore, A. (1998, May 25). Should schools be wired to the internet? Yes—it's essential to the way kids learn. *TIME, 151*(20). Accessed at www.cnn.com/ALLPOLITICS/1998/05/18/time /yes.html on June 26, 2020.

Gough, P. B., & Hillinger, M. L. (1980). Learning to read: An unnatural act. *Bulletin of the Orton Society, 30,* 179–196.

Grabianowski, E. (2008, July 1). *How cave dwellers work.* Accessed at https://history.howstuff works.com/historical-figures/cave-dweller.htm on March 6, 2020.

Graff, G. (2003). *Clueless in academe: How schooling obscures the life of the mind.* New Haven, CT: Yale University Press.

Greene, B. (2012, February). *Is our universe the only universe?* [Video file]. Accessed at www.ted .com/talks/brian_greene_is_our_universe_the_only_universe/transcript on April 4, 2020.

Grice, H. P. (1975). Logic and conversation. In P. Cole & J. L. Morgan (Eds.), *Syntax and semantics: Speech acts* (Vol. 3, pp. 41–58). New York: Academic Press.

Hanford, E. (2018, September 10). *Hard words: Why aren't kids being taught to read?* Accessed at www.apmreports.org/story/2018/09/10/hard-words-why-american-kids-arent-being-taught -to-read on March 6, 2020.

Hardy, J. (2016, September 15). *A history of ebooks.* Accessed at https://historycooperative.org /a-history-of-e-books on March 6, 2020.

Harford, T. (2017, March 13). *How the invention of paper changed the world.* Accessed at www.bbc.com/news/the-reporters-38892687 on March 6, 2020.

Harris, J. (1836). *Peter Piper's practical principles of plain and perfect pronunciation.* London: Author.

Hart, B., & Risley, T. R. (1995). *Meaningful differences in the everyday experience of young American children.* Baltimore, MD: Paul H. Brookes.

Heckelman, R. G. (1969). A neurological-impress method of remedial-reading instruction. *Academic Therapy, 4*(4), 277–283.

Heitin, L. (2016, October 11). *Cultural Literacy* creator carries on campaign. *Education Week, 36*(8), 1, 12.

Heller, J. (1961). *Catch-22.* New York: Simon & Schuster.

Hinton, S. E. (1967). *The outsiders.* New York: Viking.

Hirsch, E. D., Jr. (1987). *Cultural literacy: What every American needs to know.* Boston: Houghton Mifflin.

Hirsch, E. D., Jr. (2003). Reading comprehension requires knowledge—of words and the world. *American Educator, 27*(1), 10–13, 16–22, 28–29, 48.

Hirsch, E. D., Jr. (2006, April 25). Reading-comprehension skills? What are they really? *Education Week.* Accessed at www.edweek.org/ew/articles/2006/04/26/33hirsch.h25.html on March 6, 2020.

Hirsch, E. D., Jr. (2018). *Why knowledge matters: Rescuing our children from failed educational theories.* Cambridge, MA: Harvard Education Press.

History-Computer.com. (n.d.). *Ángela Ruiz Robles.* Accessed at https://history-computer.com /Dreamers/Robles.html on March 6, 2020.

Hochman, J. C., & Wexler, N. (2017). *The writing revolution: A guide to advancing thinking through writing in all subjects and grades.* San Francisco: Jossey-Bass.

Hoffer, E. (1973). *Reflections on the human condition.* New York: Harper & Row.

Hoffower, H. (2019, August 15). Millennials and Gen Z love their technology—but American seniors are actually spending the most time on their screens. *Business Insider.* Accessed at www.businessinsider.com/american-seniors-technologically-addiction-versus-millennials -gen-z-2019-8 on June 26, 2020.

Hutton, J. S., Dudley, J., Horowitz-Kraus, T., DeWitt, T., & Holland, S. K. (2019). Associations between screen-based media use and brain white matter integrity in preschool-aged children. *JAMA Pediatrics, 174*(1). Accessed at http://dx.doi.org/10.1001/jamapediatrics.2019.3869 on June 26, 2020.

Joyce, B., Calhoun, E., & Hopkins, D. (1999). *The new structure of school improvement: Inquiring schools and achieving students.* Philadelphia: Open University Press.

International Olympic Committee. (n.d.). *The Olympic motto.* Accessed at www.olympic.org/the-olympic-motto on March 6, 2020.

Ivey, G. (2002). Getting started: Manageable literacy practices. *Educational Leadership, 60*(3). Accessed at www.ascd.org/publications/educational-leadership/nov02/vol60/num03/Getting-Started@-Manageable-Literacy-Practices.aspx on March 6, 2020.

Jabr, F. (2013, April 11). The reading brain in the digital age: The science of paper versus screens. *Scientific American.* Accessed at www.scientificamerican.com/article/reading-paper-screens on March 6, 2020.

Kaefer, T., Neuman, S. B., & Pinkham, A. M. (2015). Pre-existing background knowledge influences socioeconomic differences in preschoolers' word learning and comprehension. *Reading Psychology, 36*(3), 203–231.

Kant, I. (1998). *Critique of pure reason* (P. Guyer & A. W. Wood, Trans.). New York: Cambridge University Press. (Original work published 1781)

Korbey, H. (2018, August 21). Digital text is changing how kids read—just not in the way that you think. *MindShift.* Accessed at www.kqed.org/mindshift/49092/digital-text-is-changing-how-kids-read-just-not-in-the-way-that-you-think on March 6, 2020.

Krull, K. (2009). *The boy who invented TV: The story of Philo Farnsworth.* New York: Knopf.

La Farge, P. (2016, January 7). The deep space of digital reading: Why we shouldn't worry about leaving print behind. *Nautilus.* Accessed at http://nautil.us/issue/32/space/the-deep-space-of-digital-reading on March 6, 2020.

Layne, S. L. (2015). *In defense of read-aloud: Sustaining best practice.* Portland, ME: Stenhouse.

Lee, H. (1960). *To kill a mockingbird.* Philadelphia: Lippincott.

Lemov, D., Driggs, C., & Woolway, E. (2016). *Reading reconsidered: A practical guide to rigorous literacy instruction.* San Francisco: Jossey-Bass.

Lemov, D., Woolway, E., & Yezzi, K. (2012). *Practice perfect: 42 rules for getting better at getting better.* San Francisco: Jossey-Bass.

Leutze, E. (1851). *Washington crossing the Delaware* [Painting]. New York: Metropolitan Museum of Art.

Liu, E. (2015, July 3). What every American should know: Defining common cultural literacy for an increasingly diverse nation. *The Atlantic.* Accessed at www.theatlantic.com/politics/archive/2015/07/what-every-american-should-know/397334 on March 6, 2020.

Liu, Z. (2005). Reading behavior in the digital environment: Changes in reading behavior over the past ten years. *Journal of Documentation, 61*(6), 700–712.

Longfellow, H. W. (1909). *Hiawatha*. Chicago: Reilly and Britton.

Lovely, S. (2019, September 23). 10 brilliant hard science fiction novels for those who take their science fiction with a side of accuracy. *The Portalist*. Accessed at http://theportalist.com /10-brilliant-hard-science-fiction-novels on March 5, 2020.

Luscombe, B. (2019, July 22). How parents of dyslexic kids took to their statehouses and won. *TIME*. Accessed at https://time.com/5624266/dyslexia-state-legislation-fight on March 6, 2020.

MacLachlan, P. (1985). *Sarah, plain and tall*. New York: Harper & Row.

Maclean, R. (1988). Two paradoxes of phonics. *The Reading Teacher, 41*(6), 514–517.

Mangen, A., Walgermo, B. R., & Bronnick, K. (2013). Reading linear texts on paper versus computer screen: Effects on reading comprehension. *International Journal of Educational Research, 58*, 61–68. Accessed at https://educacion.udd.cl/files/2017/05/MI_MAngen-et -al-2012-Reading-linear-texts-on-paper-versus-computer-screen-effects-on-reading.pdf on March 6, 2020.

Manguel, A. (1997). *A history of reading*. New York: Penguin.

Martin, B., Jr., & Archambault, J. (1989). *Chicka chicka boom boom*. New York: Simon & Schuster.

Martin, B., Jr., & Archambault, J. (1995). *Chicka chicka boom boom: Book and CD*. New York: Simon & Schuster Interactive.

Martin, M. O., & Mullis, I. V. S. (Eds.). (2013). *TIMSS and PIRLS 2011: Relationships among reading, mathematics, and science achievement at the fourth grade—Implications for early learning*. Chestnut Hill, MA: Boston College.

Marzano, R. J. (2004). *Building background knowledge for academic achievement: Research on what works in schools*. Alexandria, VA: Association for Supervision and Curriculum Development.

Marzano, R. J. (2017). *The new art and science of teaching*. Bloomington, IN: Solution Tree Press.

McMurrer, J. (2007, December). *Choices, changes, and challenges: Curriculum and instruction in the NCLB era*. Washington, DC: Center on Education Policy.

Merton, R. K. (1968). The Matthew effect in science: The reward and communication systems of science are considered. *Science, 159*(3810), 56–63. Accessed at www.garfield.library.upenn .edu/merton/matthew1.pdf on March 6, 2020.

MetaMetrics. (n.d.). *Compare Lexile measures with grade levels*. Accessed at https://lexile.com /educators/measuring-growth-with-lexile/lexile-measures-grade-equivalents on June 26, 2020.

Mumford, T. (2015, October 27). *Who really wrote "It was a dark and stormy night"?* Accessed at www.mprnews.org/story/2015/10/27/bcst-books-dark-and-stormy-night on June 22, 2020.

Myracle, J., Kingsley, B., & McClellan, R. (2019, March 7). We have a national reading crisis. *Education Week.* Accessed at www.edweek.org/ew/articles/2019/03/07/we-have-a-national -reading-crisis.html on April 13, 2020.

Nabokov, V. (1959). *Invitation to a beheading* (D. Nabokov, Trans.). New York: Random House.

Nagy, W. E., & Herman, P. A. (1984, October). *Limitations of vocabulary instruction* (Technical Report No. 326). Champaign, IL: Center for the Study of Reading. Accessed at www.ideals .illinois.edu/handle/2142/17599 on April 3, 2020.

National Aphasia Association. (n.d.a). *Broca's (expressive) aphasia.* Accessed at www.aphasia.org /aphasia-resources/brocas-aphasia on March 6, 2020.

National Aphasia Association. (n.d.b). *Wernicke's (receptive) aphasia.* Accessed at www.aphasia .org/aphasia-resources/wernickes-aphasia on March 6, 2020.

National Center for Education Statistics. (n.d.a). *NAEP report card: Reading—Grade 4.* Accessed at www.nationsreportcard.gov/reading/nation/scores/?grade=4 on August 24, 2020.

National Center for Education Statistics. (n.d.b). *NAEP report card: Reading—Grade 8.* Accessed at www.nationsreportcard.gov/reading/nation/scores/?grade=8 on August 24, 2020.

National Center for Education Statistics. (n.d.c). *NAEP report card: Reading—Grade 12.* Accessed at www.nationsreportcard.gov/reading/nation/scores/?grade=12 on August 24, 2020.

National Center for Education Statistics. (2013). *Table 221.30: Average National Assessment of Educational Progress (NAEP) reading scale score and percentage distribution of students, by age, amount of reading for school and for fun, and time spent on homework and watching TV/video: Selected years, 1984 through 2012.* Accessed at https://nces.ed.gov/programs/digest/d15/tables /dt15_221.30.asp on June 26, 2020.

National Governors Association Center for Best Practices & Council of Chief State School Officers. (2010). *Common Core State Standards for English language arts and literacy in history/ social studies, science, and technical subjects.* Washington, DC: Authors. Accessed at www.core standards.org/assets/CCSSI_ELA%20Standards.pdf on April 11, 2020.

Newton, I. (1846). *Newton's principia: The mathematical principles of natural philosophy.* Accessed at https://en.wikisource.org/wiki/Page:Newton%27s%_Principia_(1846).djvu/89 on March 30, 2020.

Nin, A. (1974). *The diary of Anaïs Nin, 1947–1955.* San Diego, CA: Harcourt Brace Jovanovich.

No Child Left Behind (NCLB) Act of 2001, Pub. L. No. 107-110, § 115, Stat. 1425 (2002).

NRK. (2007, February 26). *Medieval help desk with English subtitles* [Video file]. Accessed at www.youtube.com/watch?v=pQHX-SjgQvQ on March 6, 2020.

Ogle, D. M. (1986). K-W-L: A teaching model that develops active reading of expository text. *The Reading Teacher, 39*(6), 564–570.

Ottolenghi, C. (2002). *Jack and the beanstalk.* Greensboro, NC: Carson-Dellosa.

Paul, T. (1992). *National reading study and theory of reading practice.* Madison, WI: Institute for Academic Excellence.

Paul, T. (2003). *Guided independent reading: An examination of the Reading Practice Database and the scientific research supporting guided independent reading as implemented in Reading Renaissance.* Wisconsin Rapids, WI: Renaissance Learning.

Perkins, D. (1992). *Smart schools: Better thinking and learning for every child.* New York: Free Press.

Perkins-Gough, D. (2002). RAND report on reading comprehension. *Educational Leadership, 60*(3), 92.

Pimentel, S. (2018, October 26). Why doesn't every teacher know the research on reading instruction? *Education Week.* Accessed at www.edweek.org/ew/articles/2018/10/29/why -doesnt-every-teacher-know-the-research.html on March 6, 2020.

Project Gutenberg. (n.d.). *Michael S. Hart.* Accessed at www.gutenberg.org/wiki/Michael_S ._Hart on June 26, 2020.

Quammen, D. (2012). *Spillover: Animal infections and the next human pandemic.* New York: Norton.

Rea, A. (2020, January). *Reading through the ages: Generational reading survey.* Accessed at www.libraryjournal.com/?detailStory=Reading-Through-the-Ages-Generational-Reading -Survey on June 26, 2020.

Recht, D. R., & Leslie, L. (1988). Effect of prior knowledge on good and poor readers' memory of text. *Journal of Educational Psychology, 80*(1), 16–20.

Renaissance Learning. (n.d.). *Unpublished raw data.* Wisconsin Falls, WI: Author.

Renaissance Learning. (2015). *The research foundation for Accelerated Reader 360.* Wisconsin Rapids, WI: Author.

Renaissance Learning. (2016). *What kids are reading: And the path to college and careers.* Wisconsin Rapids, WI: Author.

Repoussoir. (n.d.). In *Wikipedia.* Accessed at https://en.wikipedia.org/wiki/Repoussoir on April 10, 2020.

Rodgers, R., & Hammerstein, O., II. (1965). Do-re-mi. On *The sound of music* [Soundtrack]. Camden, NJ: RCA Victor.

Romeo, C., Segaran, J., Leonard, J., Robinson, S., West, M., Mackey, A., et al. (2018, September). Language exposure relates to structural neural connectivity in childhood. *Journal of Neuroscience, 38*(36), 7870–7877. Accessed at https://doi.org/10.1523/JNEUROSCI .0484-18.2018 on June 26, 2020.

Routman, R. (1991). *Invitations: Changing as teachers and learners K–12.* Portsmouth, NH: Heinemann.

Sagan, C., Druyan, A., & Soter, S. (Writers). (1980). *Cosmos: A personal voyage* [Television series]. Arlington, VA: Public Broadcasting Service.

Sage, K., Augustine, H., Shand, H., Bakner, K., & Rayne, S. (2019). Reading from print, computer, and tablet: Equivalent learning in the digital age. *Education and Information Technologies, 24*(4), 2477–2502.

Sanchez, C. A., & Wiley, J. (2009). To scroll or not to scroll: Scrolling, working memory capacity, and comprehending complex texts. *Human Factors: The Journal of the Human Factors and Ergonomics Society, 51*(5), 730–738. Accessed at https://doi.org/10.1177/0018720809352788 on June 26, 2020.

Schmoker, M. (2006). *Results now: How we can achieve unprecedented improvements in teaching and learning.* Alexandria, VA: Association for Supervision and Curriculum Development.

Schmoker, M. (2011). *Focus: Elevating the essentials to radically improve student learning.* Alexandria, VA: Association for Supervision and Curriculum Development.

Schmoker, M. (2018). *Focus: Elevating the essentials to radically improve student learning* (2nd ed.). Alexandria, VA: Association for Supervision and Curriculum Development.

Schneider, W., Körkel, J., & Weinert, F. E. (1989). Domain-specific knowledge and memory performance: A comparison of high- and low-aptitude children. *Journal of Educational Psychology, 81*(3), 306–312.

Schuessler, J. (2010, April 8). The godfather of the e-reader. *The New York Times.* Accessed at www.nytimes.com/2010/04/11/books/review/Schuessler-t.html?pagewanted=all&_r=0 on March 6, 2020.

Schwartz, K. (2016, October 16). Strategies to help students "go deep" when reading digitally. *MindShift.* Accessed at www.kqed.org/mindshift/46426/strategies-to-help-students-go-deep-when-reading-digitally on March 6, 2020.

Screenager. (n.d.). In *Lexico.com Online Dictionary.* Accessed at www.lexico.com/definition/screenager on June 26, 2020.

Seuss, D. (1957). *The cat in the hat.* Boston: Houghton Mifflin.

Share, D. L. (1995). Phonological recoding and self-teaching: *Sine qua non* of reading acquisition. *Cognition, 55*(2), 151–218.

Share, D. L. (1999). Phonological recoding and orthographic learning: A direct test of the self-teaching hypothesis. *Journal of Experimental Child Psychology, 72*(2), 95–129.

Sharma, S. (2018, November 4). *Different types or genres of books with examples.* Accessed at https://gladreaders.com/types-or-genres-of-books on April 4, 2020.

Singer, L. M., & Alexander, P. A. (2017). Reading on paper and digitally: What the past decades of empirical research reveal. *Review of Educational Research, 87*(6), 1007–1041.

Silverstein, S. (1964). *The giving tree.* New York: Harper & Row.

Silverstein, S. (1974). *Where the sidewalk ends.* New York: HarperCollins.

Simms, J. A., & Marzano, R. J. (2019). *The new art and science of teaching reading.* Bloomington, IN: Solution Tree Press.

Singer, L. M., & Alexander, P. A. (2017). Reading on paper and digitally: What the past decades of empirical research reveal. *Review of Educational Research, 87*(6), 1007–1041.

Sood, A. (2013). *The Mayo Clinic guide to stress-free living.* Boston: Da Capo Press.

Sparks, D. (2005). *Leading for results: Transforming teaching, learning, and relationships in schools.* Thousand Oaks, CA: Corwin Press.

Sparks, S. D. (2016, May 16). *Screens vs. print: Does digital reading change how students get the big picture?* [Blog post]. Accessed at http://blogs.edweek.org/edweek /inside-school-research/2016/05/does_digital_reading_change_comprehension.html on April 10, 2020.

Spill. (n.d.). In *Merriam-Webster's online dictionary.* Accessed at www.merriam-webster.com /dictionary/spill on April 3, 2020.

Stanovich, K. E. (1986). Matthew effects in reading: Some consequences of individual differences in the acquisition of literacy. *Reading Research Quarterly, 21*(4), 360–407.

Stanovich, K. E. (1988). Explaining the differences between the dyslexic and the garden-variety poor reader: The phonological-core variable-difference model. *Journal of Learning Disabilities, 21*(10), 590–604.

Stanovich, K. E., & West, R. F. (1989). Exposure to print and orthographic processing. *Reading Research Quarterly, 24*(4), 402–433.

Steiner, D. (2017). *Curriculum research: What we know and where we need to go.* Accessed at http://standardswork.org/wp-content/uploads/2017/03/sw-curriculum-research-report-fnl.pdf on March 27, 2020.

Stiggins, R. J. (2017). *The perfect assessment system.* Alexandria, VA: Association for Supervision and Curriculum Development.

Storyline Online. (2012, May 21). *Wilfrid Gordon McDonald Partridge read by Bradley Whitford* [Video file]. Accessed at www.storylineonline.net/books/wilfrid-gordon-mcdonald-partridge on April 27, 2020.

Sullivan, S. A., & Puntambekar, S. (2015). Learning with digital texts: Exploring the impact of prior domain knowledge and reading comprehension ability on navigation and learning outcomes. *Computers in Human Behavior, 50*, 299–313. Accessed at https://doi.org/10.1016 /j.chb.2015.04.016 on June 26, 2020.

Sylwester, R. (1995). *A celebration of neurons: An educator's guide to the human brain.* Alexandria, VA: Association for Supervision and Curriculum Development.

Tatter, G. (2016, March 14). *Parents push for more screening, support for students with dyslexia.* Accessed at https://chalkbeat.org/posts/tn/2016/03/14/parents-push-for-more-screening -support-for-students-with-dyslexia on April 11, 2020.

Tierney, R. J., Anders, P. L., & Mitchell, J. N. (Eds.). (1987). *Understanding readers' understanding: Theory and practice.* New York: Routledge.

Topping, K. J. (2001). Paired Reading with peers and parents: Factors in effectiveness and new developments. In C. Harrison & M. Coles (Eds.), *The reading for real handbook* (2nd ed., pp. 145–165). New York: Routledge.

Topping, K. J., & Paul, T. (2011). Computer-assisted assessment of practice at reading: A large scale survey using Accelerated Reader data [Abstract]. *Reading and Writing Quarterly, 15*(3). Accessed at www.tandfonline.com/doi/abs/10.1080/105735699278198 on June 26, 2020.

Topping, K. J., Samuels, J., & Paul, T. (2007). Computerized assessment of independent reading: Effects of implementation quality on achievement gain. *School Effectiveness and School Improvement: An International Journal of Research, Policy and Practice, 18*(2), 191–208.

Trelease, J. (2013). *The read-aloud handbook: Includes a giant treasury of great read-aloud books* (7th ed.). New York: Penguin.

Twain, M. (2013). *The adventures of Huckleberry Finn.* New York: Signet Classics. (Original work published 1884)

Twenge, J. M., Martin, G. N., & Spitzberg, B. H. (2019). Trends in U.S. adolescents' media use, 1976–2016: The rise of digital media, the decline of TV, and the (near) demise of print. *Psychology of Popular Media Culture, 8*(4), 329–345.

UShistory.org. (n.d.). *The Gettysburg address.* Accessed at www.ushistory.org/documents/gettysburg.htm on April 1, 2020.

van Laar, E., van Deursen, A. J. A. M., van Dijk, J. A G. M., & de Haan, J. (2020, January). Determinants of 21st-century skills and 21st-century digital skills for workers: A systematic literature review. *SAGE Open, 10*(1). Accessed at http://journals.sagepub.com/doi/full/10.1177/2158244019900176 on June 26, 2020.

Vermeer, J. (1666–1668). *The art of painting* [Painting]. Vienna, Austria: Kunsthistorisches Museum.

Vygotsky, L. (1986). *Thought and language* (A. Kozulin, Trans.). Cambridge, MA: MIT Press.

Watson, S. (2019, October 16). *The 44 sounds in the English language.* Accessed at www.thoughtco.com/sounds-in-english-language-3111166 on March 6, 2020.

Webb, N. L. (1999). *Alignment of science and mathematics standards and assessments in four states* (Research Monograph No. 18). Washington, DC: Council of Chief State School Officers.

Weiss, D. (2017, December 2). *The essential elements of digital literacy for the 21 century workforce.* Accessed at https://enabley.io/the-essential-elements-of-digital-literacy-for-the-21st-century-workforce-infographic/ on June 26, 2020.

Wexler, N. (2018, April 13). Why American students haven't gotten better at reading in 20 years. *The Atlantic.* Accessed at www.theatlantic.com/education/archive/2018/04/-american-students-reading/557915 on March 6, 2020.

Wexler, N. (2019). *The knowledge gap: The hidden cause of America's broken education system—and how to fix it.* New York: Avery.

Wilde, R. (2019, April 26). *A beginner's guide to the French Revolution*. Accessed at www.thoughtco.com/beginners-guide-to-the-french-revolution-1221900 on April 15, 2020.

Wiliam, D. (2018). *Creating the schools our children need: Why what we're doing now won't help much (and what we can do instead)*. West Palm Beach, FL: Learning Sciences International.

Willingham, D. T. (2008). Ask the cognitive scientist: What is developmentally appropriate practice? *American Educator, 32*(2), 34–39.

Willingham, D. T. (2017). *The reading mind: A cognitive approach to understanding how the mind reads*. San Francisco: Jossey-Bass.

Willingham, D. T., & Lovette, G. (2014, September 26). Can reading comprehension be taught? *Teachers College Record*. Accessed at www.danielwillingham.com/uploads/5/0/0/7/5007325/willingham&lovette_2014_can_reading_comprehension_be_taught_.pdf on March 6, 2020.

Willis, J. (2016, November 22). *Want children to pay attention? Stimulate their curiosity*. Accessed at https://npjscilearncommunity.nature.com/users/20252-judy-willis/posts/13446-want-children-to-pay-attention-stimulate-their-curiosity on March 6, 2020.

WISE Channel. (2013, October 25). *Stanislas Dehaene: How the brain learns to read* [Video file]. Accessed at www.youtube.com/watch?v=25GI3-kiLdo on March 6, 2020.

Witten, B. (2018). *Understanding online reading patterns: The content writer's guide*. Accessed at https://health.usf.edu/is/blog/2018/06/15/Understanding-Online-Reading-Patterns-The-Content-Writers-Guide on August 3, 2020.

Wolf, M. (2018, August 25). Skim reading is the new normal: The effect on society is profound. *The Guardian*. Accessed at www.theguardian.com/commentisfree/2018/aug/25/skim-reading-new-normal-maryanne-wolf on March 6, 2020.

Wright, B. F. (1916). *The real Mother Goose*. New York: Scholastic.

Zipke, M. (2017). Preschoolers explore interactive storybook apps: The effect on word recognition and story comprehension. *Education and Information Technologies, 22*(4), 1695–1712.

Index

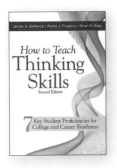

How to Teach Thinking Skills, Second Edition
James A. Bellanca, Robin J. Fogarty, and Brian M. Pete
Ensure your students develop the higher-order, complex thinking skills they need to not just survive but thrive in a 21st century world. The latest edition of this best-selling guide details a practical, three-phase teaching model and dives deep into seven essential student proficiencies.
BKF900

Metacognition
Robin J. Fogarty and Brian M. Pete
Empower your students to become mindful, reflective, and proficient thinkers and problem solvers. In *Metacognition*, authors Robin J. Fogarty and Brian M. Pete provide a practical framework to nurture these essential skills in every learner.
BKB008

The Right to Be Literate
Brian M. Pete and Robin J. Fogarty
Explore the six comprehensive skill areas essential to 21st century literacy—reading, writing, listening, speaking, viewing, and representing. Learn practical strategies for teaching students the skills they need to think critically and communicate collaboratively in the digital age.
BKF643

The New Art and Science of Teaching Reading
Julia A. Simms and Robert J. Marzano
The New Art and Science of Teaching Reading presents a compelling model for reading development structured around five key topic areas. More than 100 reading-focused instructional strategies are laid out in detail to help teachers ensure every student becomes a proficient reader.
BKF811

Wait! Your professional development journey doesn't have to end with the last pages of this book.

We realize improving student learning doesn't happen overnight. And your school or district shouldn't be left to puzzle out all the details of this process alone.

No matter where you are on the journey, we're committed to helping you get to the next stage.

Take advantage of everything from **custom workshops** to **keynote presentations** and **interactive web and video conferencing**. We can even help you develop an action plan tailored to fit your specific needs.

Let's get the conversation started.

Call 888.763.9045 today.

SolutionTree.com